Elevate from boys to MEN

Soar to New Heights in Life

Alan D. Benson

MHB Publishing

Contents

Dedication

I dedicate this book to all the boys, young men, and adult men working to find their way in life. I know firsthand how tough it can be, especially when the road ahead feels unclear, and the support you need most seems to be missing. There are times when you might feel lost, unsure of where to turn or how to even take that first step toward your goals. This book is for you – for every one of you who has ever faced doubt, felt alone, or questioned your direction.

I hope that within these pages, you will find not just guidance but also a renewed sense of purpose and unwavering encouragement to stay on the right path. This journey of becoming your best self is an ongoing process of discovery, uncovering the unique "ingredients" that make you who you are and learning how to combine them into a powerful recipe for success and fulfillment. Remember, you are not alone in this endeavor. Keep pushing forward, keep learning, and keep believing in the incredible man you are destined to become.

Acknowledgments

T hank you for picking up *Elevate – From Boys to MEN*. I wrote this book to help you better understand who you are and to provide a blueprint for mapping out a course of action to take control of your life and destiny. Creating a map can be challenging because we all face obstacles that can derail us and prevent us from achieving success. These challenges often stem from our experiences growing up. The guidance we receive from our fathers, mothers, teachers, coaches, and peers has a significant impact on who we become as men. Those who influence us can offer positive insights and essential life lessons, or they can create harmful experiences and be discouraging. All these factors shape our journey and test our character. Navigating through life can be confusing due to the temptations of what we perceive as beneficial. As you grow and mature, it's essential to learn how to be responsible—this includes maintaining a job, having a place to live, taking care of yourself, and perhaps even caring for a family. To be accountable, you need to adopt a mindset that is focused on giving your best in everything you do. I emphasize the best because, in reality, few people outside of your loved ones will care about your successes or failures. That's why it's crucial to prioritize your dreams, ambitions, and life goals.

This is my sixth book, and my driving force behind each one is my fervent desire to see you, the reader, in a better place in your life, relationships, and career. Whether teaching, advising, or consulting, I continually strive to help others. This passion fuels my writing, and I hope my experiences and insights can help illuminate your path.

My life has been filled with many wins and losses. The wins taught me humility, and the losses were valuable lessons on how to move forward. These losses were not necessarily failures, but moments of self-discovery and growth. I've discovered that my life involves learning, directing, and redirecting so I can live within my purpose. For these reasons, I thank God for being my protector and guide in life. Without Him, I would be a ship at sea without a sail.

Throughout my life, I have built meaningful relationships. I want to start by thanking my dear friend and fraternity brother, Carlos. Every time we talk, you share words of wisdom. I also want to thank my childhood friend, Robert. Brother, even though we are miles apart, our connection feels close whenever we speak. The man I am today is a direct result of my father—Sam D. Benson's—discipline, guidance, and shaping, for which I hold him in deep gratitude and respect. Dad was a disciplinarian who set expectations for me as I grew up. He was the breadwinner and provider for our family. Though not a loud man, his actions spoke loudly and clearly. But he would not have been the man he was without the support of my mother, Marthella Benson. Mom gained her wings in September 2016, but her teachings and legacy live on. I miss and love you, Mom! Thank you for being a woman of faith and service!

I want to thank the men of Alpha Phi Alpha Fraternity, Inc. Being made an Alpha over 36 years ago was a blessing to me. This fraternity further solidified in me the idea of how men should act to be successful in the classroom, in their profession, serve the community, and respect women. The principles and values I learned from this fraternity have shaped my life and work. Over the years, I have met dynamic men from various professions and walks of life who are doing great work. Keep marching toward the light, my brothers.

I am always mindful that whatever I do or achieve is not solely due to my efforts. Therefore, I want to express my deepest gratitude to my brother, Ray, and my sisters, Janet, Pam, and Stephanie. Our conversations, laughter, and prayers resonate deeply in my soul, and I love each of you for your encouragement, constructive criticism, and humor. We are family! I would also like to thank my love and wife, Debbie. When I look out at the crowd, the first person I see is always you. You are my biggest supporter, my rock, and the very foundation I stand on. You have this incredible ability to keep me going, to inject me with energy and perspective, even when I feel absolutely drained and exhausted. You don't just cheer *for* me; you give me the strength to *keep running the race*. Please keep cheering, because your voice is the one I need to hear the most!

Preface

*E*levate — *From Boys to MEN* is a book that provides boys with a roadmap for transitioning from boyhood to manhood. It outlines best practices for boys to evolve into the men they aspire to be. They will gain insights into how making responsible decisions and cultivating a positive attitude can help them achieve their life goals. Additionally, they will discover that developing strong values, respect, and integrity is vital for achieving success. The journey from boyhood to manhood is not always straightforward, but with this book as a guide, boys can pursue their dreams and discover what it takes to become their best selves. They will learn the significance of having a sense of purpose and resilience to remain focused on their chosen path. They will also discover how cultivating good habits, such as self-discipline, respect, and hard work, will contribute to their growth as men.

I believe this is an invaluable guide for males of all ages seeking guidance on becoming men of integrity, honor, and success. The examples provided will empower them to become responsible adults who can reach their full potential. They will gain the confidence and courage to lead meaningful lives and make a positive impact on their families, communities, and society.

This book also offers a unique perspective that encourages boys to pursue their dreams while remaining open to various experiences. It enables them to understand the importance of taking risks to shape their futures and to have a meaningful impact in their communities and society. It guides them to strike a balance between taking the right risks and staying true to themselves. It teaches them how to make wise decisions and develop a strong sense of identity, as well as the courage and resilience necessary for success in all areas of life.

Times have changed in many ways over the last few decades, and our lifestyles have undergone significant evolution. One important change is the development and advancement of technology and artificial intelligence (AI). Its impact on teenagers has been both positive and negative. Access to information and task efficiency have improved, and social media has created a new layer of reality through technology. This reality, whether real or perceived, has positioned teenage boys to become influencers. Conversely, social media has also created a platform for bullying, which has heightened anxiety and depression among the young and has also increased suicide rates.

Another change is the rise in single-parent households led by mothers. This has transformed the way parents and children interact socially. I firmly believe that children, both girls and boys, need the support and nurturing of both a positive man and a woman, because there are traits that only a man can teach a boy, and that only a woman can teach a girl.

I raise this point about the increase in single-parent households because the household serves as a child's foundation and socialization hub. I am not suggesting that a child raised in a single-parent home is destined for failure. I do believe, however, that both boys and girls need positive influences to help them gain the confidence to flourish and succeed in this society. Both men and women play essential roles in nurturing a boy, for example, because each brings a unique perspective. In my view, teenage boys must:

- Learn to be self-reliant: Every teenage boy should learn to take responsibility and become self-sufficient. This includes being capable of handling everyday tasks such as grocery shopping, doing laundry, cooking, cleaning the house, mowing the lawn, and changing car tires.

- Learn how to earn money and develop financial literacy: Understanding money management fundamentals is crucial for a successful life.

This may involve creating a budget, comprehending credit, and saving.

- Possess practical communication skills: Effectively communicating with all types of people is invaluable. Cultivating the ability to actively listen, articulate one's opinion, and collaborate with others is a significant asset.

- Plan their lives and tasks: Considering the future and making decisions that affect their lives is invaluable for teenage boys.

- Have confidence. Learning to be confident in one's abilities is an excellent trait. Having faith in one's opinions and standing up for oneself is also a valuable asset.

- Recognize the significance of healthy living: Every teenage boy should adopt a healthy lifestyle, which encompasses both physical and mental well-being. This involves cultivating nutritious eating habits, engaging in regular exercise, and avoiding detrimental habits like smoking and excessive drinking.

This book highlights the significance of self-awareness in a boy's life. It encourages them to understand themselves, their families, and their communities, and to recognize their strengths and weaknesses. This self-awareness is fundamental to personal growth and essential for making informed decisions and coping with life's challenges.

For young men to gain a sense of direction in life, they must understand who they are as individuals and have the support and resources to pursue their destiny. Having this support would cushion the blows that life throws at them. We must continue to push forward; quitting is not an option. All of us must keep marching forward to be the best we can be.

Let *Elevate — From Boys to MEN* be your trusted guide as you endeavor to become responsible young adults and men. My hope is that you and your parents will gain invaluable insights into what it takes to make wise decisions, stay focused on your goals, and create the future you desire. May it also help inspire you to be true to yourself while making a positive impact in the world. My goal is for you to feel equipped with the knowledge you need to achieve your dreams as you transition from boyhood to manhood.

Introduction

In January 2013, I was at home making a homemade pizza. It was about 30 degrees outside, and I was looking forward to a peaceful evening watching TV and relaxing. While preparing it, I watched videos on my computer. As I was watching, I started to feel a little dizzy. I thought it was nothing, and I stepped out to the back porch for some fresh air, but the dizziness worsened. I called my father as a precaution to let him know I wasn't feeling my best and would call him later. The dizziness intensified, and I began to panic. I felt like I was about to die because I had never experienced anything like it. I called my father again and asked him to come over immediately. I stumbled to the door to unlock it, then staggered back to the restroom, throwing up all over the place. I didn't know what was going on. My father and other family members rushed over. I couldn't understand what was happening, which made me feel it was a life-threatening situation. I stumbled to the bed and lay down.

While in bed, I noticed that the dizziness stopped when I turned my head to one side; however, it continued when I turned it to the other side. My father sat beside the bed, and I began to calm down. As I lay there, I reflected on my life growing up, wondering if I was going to die. I told my father, "Dad, thanks for providing me with a simple and good life." He told me that he had merely done what he was supposed to do as a man. He later took me to the hospital, where I discovered I had vertigo. Vertigo is a condition of the inner ear that can instantaneously throw you off balance. I went through therapy to manage and combat this ailment, which still affects me today.

Whenever we find ourselves in a life-threatening situation, our lives sometimes flash before our eyes as we recall significant moments. For me, those moments occurred in my teenage years. Becoming a teenager marked the beginning of my self-discovery. My teenage years were in the 1980s, when life was simpler than it is today. Looking back, I can see it was a good life; I had my needs met, some of my wants fulfilled, and friends around me. I didn't have to worry about any chaos. My biggest concerns were whether I would make the football team, be on the mile relay track team, and win the heart of the girl I wanted as my girlfriend. Although I considered life simple back then, I had certain expectations to meet. I had chores, like mowing the lawn and whatever else my parents asked me to do. I didn't see it as difficult because those were my responsibilities, and I respected my parents. There were some chores I didn't like, of course, but I never complained aloud, because I was a child, and they were adults.

Some looking in from the outside might have thought that my life was overly structured and even that I had a silver spoon in my mouth. But that was far from the truth, because we made do with what we had. We weren't millionaires, but I was raised with many values and principles for living. Those values and principles still resonate with me today, and I have incorporated many of them into raising my own children because I knew they were essential for thriving in this society.

We all have our own set of values. Some of mine include living a Christian life and treating others the way I want to be treated. Other important values for me are being responsible, working hard, and leading by example. These are principles for living—habits that align with my values. For instance, I was taught not to make hasty decisions, but to consider the overall costs, whether financial or personal. This is true, for example, when purchasing a home and weighing the costs against the benefits. Another principle instilled in me is to save for a rainy day. There will be good times and bad, so it's important to have money set aside for those uncertain times. Losing a job without any savings can be difficult and lead to tough times, but if you have savings, life's pressures might not weigh as heavily on you as they would if your bank account were empty.

I have been in direct contact with teenagers, young men, and adult men for many years, both within my family and in various settings, including church, work, and my community. I make it a point to always share a little wisdom with them in a respectful way. This is because I have high expectations for them as men, and if I witness them doing something out of line, I believe they should be accountable. For example, while working at Kentucky State University, I kindly asked young male students with their pants sagging to pull them up. I explained that they were on a college campus and should carry themselves more respectfully. Correcting and asking young men to pull their pants up became so frequent that when some saw me walking in their direction, they would say, "I know, I know, I'm pulling them up." Their reactions and my encouragement made me feel I was establishing a standard for them to follow.

I have these expectations for teenagers and young men because I want you to carry yourself with high regard in a respectable way. I know that life will deliver some blows to you that you might not understand. We are all made differently, and some of you will embrace these setbacks as a challenge, while others will lose hope because you don't know where to turn or don't have a support system in place. But please listen when I say that, regardless of your circumstance, whatever you are going through won't last forever if you keep your head up, have courage, faith, and work through the issue. We are all here for a purpose, but it's up to us to figure out that purpose so we can be the best men we can be. That is why I wrote this book.

Elevate – From Boys to MEN is a book that provides habit-forming strategies for teenage boys, young men, and men seeking to revamp their lives. This book is meant to do two things: First, to define and outline how a responsible man acts through his actions. I offer strategies for transforming thoughts into actions to become the man you want to be. A man driven by character, not societal influences. Through character, you will be motivated to create a sustainable path in your life and earn the income necessary to be self-sufficient, and if you have a family and children, to support them. This does not mean you won't face challenges and setbacks in life, but you will be better able to weather life's storms with proper planning and faith. The second thing this book is meant to do is to share my story—the challenges, defeats, and victories I encountered while coming into my own. My life experiences have given me a greater awareness and appreciation of the blessings God has bestowed upon me. My hope in sharing my story is that it will help readers face their own obstacles and will offer a different perspective on how to handle them. My goal is for every reader to purposefully utilize the content to enhance their own lives and the lives of those around them.

My wish is for you to open your mind to discover your purpose, embrace manhood, and map your life with focus and intention. This book is a change agent that will help you be more responsible in everything you do. It can be an awakening for you to shine and be the best man you can be. Regardless of your circumstances, you were born with talents that can help you prosper. That does not mean life will always be easy. There will be disappointments and moments you cannot explain. We all experience them. But whatever you are going through, whether good or bad times, you must keep your head up and filter out the noise to maintain who you are as a man, and have the fortitude to seek help, maintain your focus, and keep moving forward. Remember, adversity in life is not an obstacle but an opportunity to change your circumstances. But to do so, you must know who you are and what you are made of as a man. You must understand your strengths and weaknesses and develop a plan for what you seek to accomplish and where you want to go.

Please note that while this book is primarily intended for teenage boys maturing into men and young adult males, it also addresses older men who are not behaving as men. I realize there are numerous reasons for this, but I also know it is never too late to be the best man you can be by being more responsible and self-sufficient.

As you reflect on your life so far, there have doubtless been times when you did not have all the answers, and this will continue to be true as you grow into a man. This is why I believe this book is essential as you seek to:

- Own up to your responsibilities and hold yourself accountable.

- Live within your purpose.

- Map out a new direction in life.

- Learn from your failures and keep moving.

- Become a leader in your family and community.

- Build an economic and financial foundation for yourself.

Living life to the fullest is about more than getting up every day, working, and returning home. It is about knowing and understanding your society and how it functions. I hope this book will help you better understand who you are, where you want to go, and map out a strategy for getting there. Life is not easy, but if you keep your head up and eyes open and are determined to get what you desire, you will achieve what you want. If you apply the strategies I offer here, you will step in the right direction and become the best man you can be.

A young male's productivity and focus in life often come from what his parents teach, so Chapter One focuses on parents. Having the proper upbringing can jumpstart a boy's life because, let's face it, parents can provide the tools and direction for him to be responsible and successful.

If you are a parent reading this, you know that parenting is not easy. It takes a village to raise any child, but of course, with the high divorce rate and more and more children being born into single-parent homes, the role of fathers or male role models in a teenage boy's life is often limited. A positive father figure is critical to raising boys, but the reality is that women, from mothers to grandmothers, have been raising boys for one reason or another for decades, some with better results than others. This is why I believe that an extended family or community with positive father-figures can make all the difference in a boy's upbringing. Frankly, even if a father is present, having a community that can pour positive teachings into adolescent boys can only be beneficial to their future. In Chapter One, I will discuss the positives and negatives of parenting and what parents can do to ensure their teenage boy is taught the dos and don'ts so he will grow into a responsible man. This chapter concludes with a 12-month step-by-step plan for strengthening your son's confidence in being socially equipped and educationally prepared for life.

Understanding who we are is key to our identity. It is our foundation, much like that of a home; we want our home to be built on a solid foundation, and reinforced in the event of a storm, right? The same is true for you; when you know who you are and where you want to go, you will have a solid foundation that will help you withstand life's challenges. You will know what you stand for and where you want to go in life. Chapter Two asks the question, "Who am I?" The idea is to force you to look deep inside yourself to answer this, along with follow-up questions like, "Why am I on this earth?," "What should I do when I grow up, and will I succeed?" It is okay if you cannot answer these questions yet because this is a discovery process, and you'll have to look in the mirror and find some quiet time to reflect on past experiences and future goals.

Unleashing your purpose means silencing the noise of self-doubt, disappointment, and chaos in your life. To do this, you need to establish goals and focus on reaching them as soon as possible. No one wants to find themselves on their deathbed surrounded by the 'ghosts of opportunity,' as renowned motivational speaker Les Brown calls them. These ghosts are angry and disappointed because they were given to you to bring you a fulfilled life, but you let them die with you.[1]

Chapter Two will help you get to the core of who you are. You will learn what is driving your behavior and find out what your gifts are. You'll be asked about your core values, strengths and passions, goals, what drives you, your biggest influences, and what fulfills you. All this will tell you what you are made of as a

---

1. Clark, "Les Brown Shares His Story."

man, what areas you need to improve, and what you need to focus on to be the best man you can be.

Chapter Three is about taming your distractions and silencing the noise. We live in a vastly different world from our predecessors, and teenage boys must deal with many external and internal pressures from social media, at school and at home. This can cause them to struggle with self-esteem, which can affect their mental health and overall well-being because they feel they are not measuring up. Chapter Three includes steps to silence the noise because we all need peace. When you are at peace, you can think more clearly and make better decisions. We'll also talk about how to manage what is happening in your world by improving your time management, establishing quiet spots, and managing the use of your cell phone. Incorporating the steps in this chapter will improve your focus.

In Chapter Four, we'll discuss character. Character is the qualities that define you and your moral and ethical nature. Character is about knowing your values, being honest and respectful, and showing kindness. It determines if you are a good friend, a reliable teammate, a good worker, and a responsible mate. Character is not something we are born with; it is something we build over time. It must be taught and practiced, which takes time and effort, so being patient with yourself and celebrating your progress is essential. In this chapter, I provide you with a 30-day development plan to help you begin building strong character.

Having discipline is another critical aspect of becoming a man. You can have all the talent in the world, but you will not reach your full potential without discipline. Chapter Five is about discipline and the keys to unlocking your potential. We'll focus on the importance of discipline in achieving success in life. For example, I ran track in high school and made it my goal to qualify for the "Meet of Champions," a prestigious event for the best of the best in my community. I worked hard both in practice and outside of practice and qualified as a result of my efforts. Of course, I wanted it and enjoyed running track, so having the discipline to work on it was easy for me. But what about when you have to be disciplined in something you don't enjoy, like studying or working a job you don't like? Chapter Five includes guidance for building discipline by taking small steps, answering why, and embracing the process.

The transition from boyhood to manhood involves maturing physically, as well as mentally and emotionally. This is when you begin taking responsibility for who you are as a maturing man. In Chapter Six, I will discuss taking ownership of your future by assuming responsibility. This stage ultimately defines your identity, values, and beliefs. During this transition, it's crucial to understand and embrace responsibility by changing your mindset from dependent to independent. This means looking for ways to earn money and learning how to manage it. It means being more proactive than reactive; for example, if the lawn needs cutting, don't wait to be asked to cut it. Being consistently proactive will help you create a solid foundation of positive habits while also acknowledging negative ones. A negative habit is anything that diverts your focus from being the best man you can be. It can be drugs, alcohol, friends, relationships, and sometimes even a job.

While I was growing up, Dad would say things to me like, "Alan, it is not what you make but what you do with what you make." He told me that I had to know how to manage my money, no matter how little or how much I made. Chapter Seven is about hustling smart by taking control of your finances. When you hustle, you work hard, and your finances will grow when you do it smartly. You are never too young to start managing your money correctly, but to do so, you have to have a plan and be disciplined in executing it. To execute any financial plan, it is best to have a budget. In Chapter Seven, I will discuss the importance of budgeting and show you how to set up and monitor a budget. You will undoubtedly make mistakes, but some of the best lessons we learn come from our mistakes. I will also discuss how to get your money to start working for you so you can live a fruitful life.

What you plan to do in life defines where you want to go and who you want to be. I understand that if you're still in high school, you may not know these answers, but high school is the perfect time to explore what you like and what you aspire to become. But regardless of your age, it is never too late to go after what you aim for, so Chapter Eight focuses on forging your own path to build your career. This chapter encourages you to discover your unique talents and purpose, enabling you to create a fulfilling career. I provide sample questions for informational interviews and outline strategies for networking and cultivating professional relationships to help you advance in your chosen field.

I have been told that you cannot soar like an eagle if you're hanging around with geese, and who you hang around with, you will become. In Chapter Nine, we will discuss friends, why they matter, and why we must choose them wisely. Friends play a significant role in shaping our personality and guiding our direction in life. Your friends can influence your thoughts, actions, and decisions, both positively and negatively. Surrounding yourself with positive, supportive, and motivated individuals can inspire you to be your best self, pursue your goals, and make good choices. In this chapter, I will discuss how to handle peer pressure and bullying, as well as recognize the red flags of negative behavior. I will explain how to identify whether a friend is truly a friend, and if they are not, how to maintain a healthy distance from them.

I don't know anyone who has achieved anything solely on their own, whether it's becoming a schoolteacher, CEO, or billionaire. There's always someone who has shown interest in you and has the resources or voice to open that door of opportunity. I firmly believe that the first step to earning their respect is to show them respect first. And treating others with respect begins with self-respect. While Chapter 10 is about strengthening your relationships and understanding the power of respect, we will also learn what respect is and isn't, because respect is the foundation for all healthy relationships. This chapter includes practical steps for recognizing your worth, setting boundaries, and preventing others from taking advantage of you. Finally, you'll learn a few strategies for dealing with disrespect, empowering you to walk away from unhealthy situations when necessary.

When I was growing up, Dad would constantly emphasize the importance of having a plan in life. I understood what he meant at a young age. For example, I wanted to earn money, so I planned to shovel snow and mow lawns. My strategy was to look at neighbors whose yards needed work and ask if I could mow their lawns. I did the same thing in winter when neighbors needed sidewalks or driveways shoveled. Having a plan is essential if you have goals in life, and Chapter 11 explains how to develop one. This chapter focuses on planning your future and creating a blueprint for personal growth. It emphasizes the importance of setting goals, making plans, and taking action. We close this chapter with a 90-day plan to help you reach your goals.

Chapter Twelve is my final word on elevating yourself in life: While there are no guarantees in this life, you can overcome challenges and reach your full potential by combining a strong belief in yourself, a supportive network, and unwavering faith. Having faith in something bigger than oneself, whether it be God, a higher power, or a set of guiding principles, provides comfort, direction, and strength, particularly during difficult times. It fosters a positive mindset, allowing us to approach challenges with resilience and perseverance.

Chapter 1: Raising Responsible Men
A Message to Parents

In 2000, the Louisville Urban League hired me to lead the Campaign for African American Achievement. The campaign addressed the achievement gap between Black Americans and other races. It was also about promoting achievement matters and equipping parents to be better consumers of public education. This exciting opportunity allowed me to connect with citizens, educators, clergy, and youth to promote and advocate for the idea that achievement matters. It was a natural fit for me because my parents raised me to strive to better myself educationally, and attending college was a given in the Benson household. This important role also allowed me to meet and develop relationships with executive educators of the school system, businesspeople, parents, community advocates, and many others who came together for a common goal: to put in place strategies, advocate for policies, and equip parents to be the best parents they could be by ensuring that their children received a quality education. We had parent meetings at churches and education summits, where national educators discussed their strategies for turning around underperforming schools. People were vigilant because they knew the importance of a quality education.

Being the head of the Campaign of African American Achievement prepared me to raise and prepare my own children to be the best they can be in life. It gave me a new perspective on the educational system, how to navigate it, and how I would raise my children. During my time at the Louisville Urban League, my then-wife, Doris, and I had twins, Hilton and Hayley. We wanted the best for them from birth and made sure they received the best possible education. They excelled academically, but that was the expectation Doris and I had of them.

Hilton and Hayley are now college graduates with high ambitions for their careers. People who know me often say that I am proud of them, and I am pleased, but the truth is, I'm more than proud; I am very grateful that they have remained focused and done the right thing while in school. I know our lives could change at any moment in this society, so I always encourage Hilton and Hayley to lead a prayerful life, do the right thing, treat others how they want to be treated, and stay focused. Life is a gift, and we have a purpose, so we must maximize our purpose by being the best we can be.

Why Is Parenting So Important to a Child's Upbringing?

I am an entrepreneur and educator. I know every child can learn with the right tools and support to help them understand and succeed. Do we have different skills? Of course. Some subjects might be more straightforward or complicated for some than they are for others. For instance, I am not a scientist, and my education reflects that. During training over the years, while covering the agendas, I would joke that I was not a physicist, so I would not be teaching this topic. The message was that I would not introduce a subject about which I was unaware.

The key for any child to learn is the instruction and support they receive from their parents. Let's face it, children pattern their lives after their parents and environment. As parents, we provide the tools our children need to learn and succeed. We serve as role models and guides, helping our children develop skills, values, and behaviors that will shape their future. Good parenting can give children a strong foundation for success, while poor parenting can hinder their development and potential. For instance, when I was in the first grade, my teacher told my mother that I was not catching on to the material like the other students, and she was thinking about sitting me in a corner. My mother told her politely and directly that she would not be putting me in any corner. My teacher got the message and did not set me apart from my classmates.

From that point on, Mom began to have me read every day before I left for school, from first grade all the way through high school. Looking back, I know it was taxing on her to do that every morning before I left for school, but she did it because it was her responsibility. Even beyond that, it showed her love for me and how much she wanted me to be able to read proficiently. As parents, we all make sacrifices for our children, so they grow and flourish in life, and this was what my mother did for me.

As we all know, there are parents out there who are not good. Can we fault them? In some cases, yes, but in others, no. Some parents are only doing what they know—what they themselves were taught, so they might not know how to raise a child. For example, suppose a child is raised in an environment where everyone is hopeless, and no one is trying to better themselves because they feel beaten down by society. In such cases, there will be mental blocks that hinder them from striving to improve their lives. Now add a baby to the equation. If that child grows up in this atmosphere without any positive influences or without learning what society can offer them, the cards will be stacked against them. Even so, we must not count them out. I have family members, friends, and associates who came from less-than-perfect situations, and yet through faith and hard work, they made it and are successful today.

Is Parenting Today the Same as It Was in the Past?

I grew up in a household with a father and mother. Most would call it a traditional household. There were rules and expectations; as a child, I respected adults and did what I was told. My father's role was to work and provide for the family, and my mother was the nurturer to five children – three girls and two boys, of which I was the youngest. She maintained the household. I was blessed because all my needs and even some of my wants were met. I did not know if I was rich or poor because life was good to me in my world.

Today, I am many years removed from childhood, and we all know that parenting has significantly transformed over the last few decades. Social shifts, economic realities, and even technological advancements have affected how children are raised today as compared to past generations. This evolution can be seen in family structures, parenting styles, and the very concept of childhood itself.

The Shift in Parenting Styles

I was born in the late 60s and grew up in an era where discipline was the dominant parenting style. This style continued in the 1960s, 70s, and early 80s. We did not question our parents' authority because it was about having respect and being obedient. My father commanded respect, and when he told us to do something, we'd better do it. Dad often said, "If you cannot abide by the rules and regulations of the house, you need to find another place to live." We not only respected our father, but we also respected our mother and all adults. Even in our neighborhood, other parents had license to discipline me. This form of discipline is carried over into schools. The principal and teachers commanded respect and discipline; if you got out of line, you would be given a paddling. That is how it was back then.

Today's parents are increasingly adopting a "conscious parenting" approach. This emphasizes emotional intelligence, building strong relationships with children, and understanding their unique needs. It is a more nuanced and reflective style, acknowledging the complexities of individual children and seeking to raise well-rounded, emotionally healthy individuals.

The Evolving Landscape of Family Life

The traditional nuclear family, a married couple with children, is no longer the dominant model. Single-parent households, blended families, and same-sex couples are all increasingly common. This diversity calls for a more flexible and adaptable approach to parenting. In the 1960s, two-parent households accounted for around 75% of all families with children living at home. This number has steadily declined, and by 2017, it was less than half.[1] I have personally witnessed this evolution within the neighborhood I grew up in. When I was a child, most homes had two parents in them. Also, everyone was a homeowner. As we moved into the 1990s, I noticed a shift in the neighborhood, from people owning their homes to people renting homes. Of course, when some neighbors passed away, their children held on to the homes and moved back in. But some were sold to people I did not know, and they rented them out. This shift occurred in countless neighborhoods just like mine across the country, leading to a significant change in the urban landscape. Many homes are now rented, and some communities have been completely transformed as a result. Single-parent households headed by women are common, and the reasons vary. Some are divorced, others never married, and some are the primary provider for their children and have the economic means to sustain a household.

---

1. Pew Research Center, "The American Family Today."

The Double-Edged Sword of Technology

Technology has become an undeniable influence on modern parenting. On one hand, a wealth of information and resources is at our fingertips. Parents can access support and guidance from sources like educational apps and online parenting communities. It also connects their kids with information. We can stay in touch with faraway loved ones with video calls and instant messaging. We can also access vast amounts of information about child development, health, and educational resources online. Technology also offers us convenience and safety. Things like monitoring apps help us keep track of our child's location, and baby monitors allow parents to check in without disturbing their child's sleep. There are educational apps and games that can help children learn in a fun and interactive way, and a wealth of online resources for creative activities and virtual field trips, many of which have enhanced the connection between parents and children.

While technology offers many benefits to parents' lives, it also creates a number of challenges. One challenge is the amount of time kids spend in front of the computer screen. Screen time can suppress the development of social skills, and social media can contribute to feelings of inadequacy and anxiety in both parents and children. Both are significant distractions for youth. We now know that children's time in front of a screen can have negative consequences, especially if it is excessive. For starters, it affects attention and focus: Studies suggest excessive screen time can negatively impact a child's ability to focus and retain information in school. The constant stimuli and distractions from screens can interfere with their ability to concentrate on traditional classroom activities.[2] Excessive screen time also affects a child's social and emotional development. Face-to-face interaction is crucial for social and emotional learning. Overreliance on screen-based communication can hinder the development of social skills like empathy, collaboration, and conflict resolution. There are also health

---

2. Langreo, "Students Are Addicted to Screens."

concerns, as too much screen time is linked to sleep problems, eye strain, and physical inactivity. On top of all that, long periods hunched over devices can contribute to poor posture and musculoskeletal issues.

This is a problem for many schools today because it interferes with students' learning. Schools are increasingly implementing guidelines to limit screen time during class. This might involve designated tech-free zones or restrictions on specific apps or websites. Educators are also exploring alternative methods for teaching that leverage technology's strengths without relying solely on screens.

Other drawbacks to technology are cyberbullying and online predators, both of which are serious concerns that parents today must deal with. Cyberbullying is the use of technology to harass, threaten, or embarrass someone. It can be relentless, following victims everywhere online. Unlike traditional bullying, it can be anonymous and permanent, with damaging posts lingering indefinitely. Online predators are even worse, as they are adults who try to exploit children. They may pose as peers, showering a child with attention to gain their trust before manipulating them into sharing personal information or engaging in inappropriate activities.

Schools Working to Find the Right Balance

Technology can be a powerful educational tool, but finding the right balance is vital. Schools, parents, and educators all play a role in promoting responsible tech use. For example, when Hilton was in middle and high school, he loved to play Roblox with his friends. His mother and I took note of how long he would be on his computer playing the game. Eventually, we had to monitor his usage of the computer to play the game. First, he had to complete homework and show satisfactory grades. Luckily, the middle and high schools he attended implemented these same strategies that fostered a culture of digital wellness. They also created a learning environment that maximized the benefits of technology while minimizing its drawbacks.

Have Children Changed or Has Parenting Changed?

I grew up when there were more families with both parents under one roof. Of course, that did not necessarily mean everything was all right in the house. There was still abuse from parents or relatives, alcoholism, and neglect at various levels. So, obviously, having two parents in the house does not mean everything is "all good." Some parents are better off being separated from each other because of the trauma their kids are experiencing and the bad habits they are learning from them. A lot of this kind of thing was covered up when I was growing up. But abuse, if not addressed or healed, can cause the victims to pass it on to their own children, and the cycle continues if it's never remedied. This is the world we are living in, which is why today's parents face greater challenges than ever before. Juggling work, family, and personal lives can be a constant struggle, and the ever-present influence of social media adds another layer of complexity.

I travel in many circles, and often have discussions about relationships, our children and parenting. Those who are close to my age all agree that children today are different from when we grew up, but to be honest, parenting has also changed. Parents are the major contributors to the way a child is raised, how they behave, and what they aspire to be. Naturally, some children have their own unique challenges, but I see countless children who do not have the basic skills they need to be an adult: treating others with respect, working hard, knowing right from wrong, and having goals and ambitions. They don't possess the skills and values their parents should be teaching them. The reality is that some parents with children were not taught these things either, so they cannot pass them down.

So, how can we ensure children are learning the right things and developing the right mindset and value system? For starters, parents must want to be there for their children, and if that means changing their ways, so be it. We must be role models for our children. I know how difficult this might be for some parents who are battling their own demons or struggling with life's challenges, but there is help. If you're one of these parents, you can seek parental assistance at your child's school; they will gladly help. Schools recognize that parents are key to a child's success, both inside and outside the classroom. When I was in school, I remember one superintendent offered services like employment and mental health assistance for parents so they could become more involved in their child's academic life. She believed that parents must be on stable ground in order to be there for their children, and her parent meetings went from having only a few in attendance to hundreds.

When parents are empowered, they can better set their own goals, and their children can learn by observing them. They can talk openly about their goals and their steps to achieve them. Such parents would not shy away from challenges and could show their children how to overcome obstacles and learn from mistakes. They also would be able to maintain an attitude of being and doing their best. I believe that regardless of where a parent is in their own life, they want the best for their children. I'm not speaking only about academic success but about cultivating a mindset that embraces challenges, seeks continuous improvement, and strives to make meaningful accomplishments. But for all that to occur, there must be consistent involvement from the parent, so the child develops educationally and socially. Ensuring that a boy or young man develops in the best way possible will improve his overall well-being and increase the probability of his future success. Below is a breakdown of how educational and social development will improve your son's well-being:

Educational Development:

- Cognitive Skills: Education fosters critical thinking, problem-solving, creativity, and analytical abilities, all essential for navigating a complex world.

- Academic Achievement: Strong educational foundations lead to better academic performance, increased earning potential, and greater career opportunities.

- Lifelong Learning: Education nurtures a love of learning and a desire for continuous personal growth.

Social Development:

- Social Skills: Social development equips children with necessary life skills like communication, empathy, cooperation, and conflict resolution.

- Emotional Intelligence: Children must learn to understand and manage their emotions, build healthy relationships, and handle social situations effectively.

- Mental and Emotional Well-being: Strong social skills contribute to improved mental health, reduced stress levels, and increased resilience.[3]

Both educational and social development are interconnected and equally crucial for a child's holistic growth. A well-rounded education emphasizing academic learning and social-emotional development provides children with the best possible foundation for a successful and fulfilling life.

Developing your son educationally and socially should come in steps according to his age. Below is a breakdown of social and educational skills boys in different age groups need to thrive in today's society:

Ages 1-4:

Social Skills:

- Sharing and taking turns

---

3. Ballantyne, "Healing Power of Green Space," 7–9.

- Basic communication and listening

- Developing empathy and understanding others' feelings

- Learning to manage emotions (anger, frustration, etc.)

Educational Skills:

- Early language development (speaking, listening, reading readiness)

- Basic number and shape recognition

- Fine motor skills (drawing, coloring, building)

- Curiosity and exploration of the world around them

Ages 5-10:

Social Skills:

- Making and maintaining friendships

- Conflict resolution and cooperation

- Teamwork and collaboration

- Developing self-confidence and self-esteem

Educational Skills:

- Reading and writing fundamentals

- Basic math skills (addition, subtraction, simple and complex division & multiplication)

- Science exploration and critical thinking

- Problem-solving and creative thinking

Ages 11-15:

Social Skills:

- Navigating peer relationships and cliques

- Developing healthy romantic relationships

- Understanding and respecting diversity

- Responsible decision-making (alcohol, drugs, sex)

Educational Skills:

- Advanced reading and writing skills

- Complex math concepts (algebra, geometry)

- Exploring interests and potential career paths

- Time management and study skills

Ages 16-18:

Social Skills:

- Building solid relationships with adults (mentors, teachers, employers)

- Developing independence and responsibility

- Setting personal and academic goals

- Understanding consent and healthy relationships

Educational Skills:

- College or career preparation

- Advanced academic subjects (history, science, literature)

- Financial literacy and money management

- Critical thinking and analysis skills

These are just general guidelines. Every child is unique, of course, and their needs will vary. Providing support and guidance tailored to each boy's strengths and challenges is essential. Below, I have also included approaches parents can take to empower their children.

- Set Age-Appropriate Goals: Start with simple, achievable goals. For young children, this could be finishing a drawing, learning a new word, or helping with chores. Goals can become more complex as they age, like mastering a skill, reading a certain number of books, or saving for a desired purchase.

- Teach Responsibility: Teach your son to learn responsibility by having him pick up his toys and put them where they belong. As he ages, consider assigning him tasks to do around the house.

- Have Joint Goal-Setting: Involve him in the goal-setting process. Ask him what he'd like to achieve and discuss realistic steps. This fosters ownership and motivation.

- Create Visuals: Create a "goal chart" together. Use pictures or stickers to represent progress. Seeing their journey visually keeps them engaged.

- Focus on Effort: Praise your child's dedication and progress, not just the final outcome. This reinforces the importance of hard work over instant results.

- Embrace Setbacks as Learning Opportunities: Obstacles are inevitable. Help your child view difficulties as bumps in the road, not dead ends. Teach them to analyze what went wrong and adjust their strategies accordingly.

- Celebrate Milestones: Acknowledge and celebrate small victories along the way. This keeps them motivated and reinforces the value of perseverance.

- Empower Decision-Making: Offer choices within reasonable boundaries. This allows them to develop problem-solving skills and take responsibility for their actions.

- Let Them Lead Projects: Assign age-appropriate tasks and allow them to complete them independently. This builds confidence and a sense of accomplishment.

- Provide Guidance, But Avoid Taking Over: Offer support and guidance when needed, but avoid micromanaging their every move. This builds their problem-solving skills and teaches resilience.

- Offer Encouragement: Be their biggest cheerleader! Acknowledge their efforts and provide positive reinforcement.

- Celebrate Diverse Interests: Encourage exploration of different interests and activities. This will help your child discover their passions and strengths.

- Offer Opportunities for Growth: Expose your son to new experiences, like sports, clubs, or community projects. This will broaden their horizons and foster new skills.

- Every Child Is Different: Tailor your approach to your child's personality and learning style.

- Focus on intrinsic motivation: Help your child discover the internal satisfaction of achieving goals rather than relying solely on external rewards.

- Balance Is Key: Do not turn everything into a competition or a goal. Allow time for free play and unstructured exploration.

Whether these strategies are new to you or not, incorporating them into your son's life can empower him to be goal-oriented and effective. This process starts early and requires consistent effort, but the rewards for parents and sons are invaluable. Your child will achieve his goals and develop the self-confidence, resilience, and problem-solving skills needed to thrive in any situation.

As parents, we don't always get it right. But we learn from our mistakes and remind ourselves that tomorrow will be a new day. Think of today as a new day for you to give your son all he deserves. After all, his success in life depends on the deposits you place in him. Giving him what he deserves does not mean giving him material things. There has to be a balance between the material things we give them and the things we make them work for. This approach will give them a sense of responsibility, a strong work ethic, and an appreciation for what it takes to earn things. For example, a friend told me he is raising his kids so they will not be in his pocket when they are grown. For this to happen, children need guiding principles and habits to be incorporated into their lives when they're young, ensuring they are going in the right direction. Below are some guiding principles and a 12-month plan to engage your son to ensure his strong social and educational development. Of course, I recommend customizing your approach according to your son's specific needs, as these are simply general suggestions.

1. Nurture Curiosity: Encourage exploration and enthusiasm when answering questions. Provide a stimulating environment with books, puzzles, and opportunities for discovery.

2. Foster a Love of Learning: Make learning fun! Play educational games, visit museums, and celebrate achievements. Show your enthusiasm for lifelong learning.

3. Develop Strong Communication Skills: Talk, read, and listen to your

son as often as possible. Encourage him to express his thoughts and feelings.

4. Build Social-Emotional Intelligence: Teach empathy, kindness, and respect for others. Help him understand and manage his emotions.

5. Encourage Independence: Allow him to make age-appropriate choices and solve problems independently. Celebrate his successes and offer gentle guidance when needed.

6. Promote Healthy Habits: Emphasize the importance of exercise, nutrition, and sleep. These all play a crucial role in brain development and overall well-being.

7. Create a Supportive Environment: Provide a safe and loving home where he feels valued and accepted.

8. Expose Him to Diverse Experiences: Introduce him to different cultures, perspectives, and ideas. This broadens his understanding of the world.

9. Set Clear Expectations: Establish consistent rules and boundaries, but with flexibility and understanding.

10. Be a Role Model: Children learn by watching. Demonstrate the values and behaviors you want your son to embody.

Below is a 12-month plan to develop and expand on your son's social skills and educational abilities. This plan aims to give him exposure and confidence in himself and his abilities so he can be the best he can be at home, school, and in the broader community. This plan is merely a guide, so feel free to customize it according to your son's interests and abilities. We are all different in our ability to be great.

12-Month Plan for Strong Social and Educational Development

Month 1: Foundation and Exploration

- Social: Enroll in a playgroup or join a local park group, such as the Cub or Boy Scouts, for age-appropriate interaction.

- Educational: Introduce a structured learning routine, such as reading together for 15 minutes every day.

Month 2: Communication and Creativity

- Social: Encourage imaginative play with other children, focusing on turn-taking and sharing.

- Educational: Start a simple science experiment or craft project together, like building a model car or rocket, emphasizing the discovery process.

Month 3: Physical Activity and Social Interaction

- Social: Join a sports team or enroll in a dance class for physical activity and social interaction.

- Educational: Visit a local library and explore different sections, encouraging curiosity about books.

Month 4: Emotional Intelligence and Empathy

- Social: Read books about emotions and discuss how characters feel. Encourage empathy and kindness toward others.

- Educational: Introduce basic math concepts through games and everyday activities.

Month 5: Nature and Exploration

- Social: Plan a nature walk or visit a park, encouraging observation and interaction with the natural world.

- Educational: Start a simple gardening project to learn about plants and the environment.

Month 6: Community Involvement and Giving Back

- Social: Volunteer at a local animal shelter or food bank to teach the importance of helping others.

- Educational: Learn basic coding or programming concepts through age-appropriate apps or websites.

Month 7: Cultural Exploration and Diversity

- Social: Visit a museum or cultural center to learn about different cultures and traditions.

- Educational: Introduce historical figures and events through age-appropriate books and documentaries.

Month 8: Problem-Solving and Critical Thinking

- Social: Encourage independent play, allowing your son to solve problems and make choices on his own.

- Educational: Play board games that involve strategy and critical thinking.

Month 9: Technology and Digital Literacy

- Social: Introduce age-appropriate educational apps and websites that promote learning and social interaction.

- Educational: Learn about online safety and responsible technology use.

Month 10: Creativity and Expression

- Social: Encourage creative expression through drawing, painting, music, writing or other art forms.

- Educational: Introduce basic musical instruments or engage in a song-writing effort.

Month 11: Healthy Habits and Well-being

- Social: Emphasize the importance of healthy habits like exercise, sleep, and nutrition for overall well-being.

- Educational: Set aside time for reading or mindfulness activities.

Month 12: Review and Reflection

- Social: Reflect on your son's social development and identify areas for continued growth.

- Educational: Review his educational progress and adjust the plan as needed.

Remember: This general plan can be adapted to your son's individual needs and interests. The idea is to create a supportive and engaging environment that fosters social and educational growth. We all know that being a parent requires a lot of work and support. Even before I had kids, I knew it took a village to raise them. If you have support, it is a blessing. My friend Kevin would often tell me that he and his wife were blessed in raising their children because they had an extended family. Of course, not all parents have extended families, and some single parents don't even have help from the birth mother or father. I know the weight of raising children is even greater in such situations.

But regardless of your circumstances, your child is here for a reason and purpose, and we all have to muster up the strength to develop our sons so that they will strive socially and educationally. This requires setting an example and standard for him. As you make the proper deposits in him, you will put him on a course to be the best he can be. I realize that as you read this book, you may be asking, "How can I do this with all the problems I have on my shoulders?" My answer is to remind you that we all have problems. Some might be big, some small, but how we handle them is key to how we raise our children. If you need prayer, ask someone to pray for you. If you need mental help, seek out mental health services. If you need a positive male role model for your son, seek out organizations that provide mentoring. I know you can do it, so let's do it!

Chapter 2: Who Am I? Understanding Your Identity and Purpose

As we know, our social and economic upbringing, who we hang with, failures, and belief in ourselves all help to shape who we are. And as I said, parental guidance can be a difference maker. I am fortunate that my parents provided a good upbringing for me because I had a roof over my head, food on the table, and clothes. I had all my needs met and even some of my wants. Dad provided most of the financial stability for our family, and Mom was primarily the nurturer of the children and the manager of the house. That is how things were done in his era: the man was the breadwinner, and the woman was the caretaker of the children and home.

Mom, being our caretaker, knew all our ways and behaviors. She often said she had to watch me closely because I was always inquisitive. Once, she told me, I climbed into the medicine cabinet! I also took a lamp apart and plugged it into the wall. While disassembling it, I was nearly electrocuted, and if it had not been for my sister Janet grabbing me, my life would have ended at that moment. To this day, I still have a mark on my finger from the voltage going through my hand.

Even at a young age, I was driven by a strong sense of determination. Before I even knew who I was, I would gravitate toward things that I considered challenges, and depending on how strong my desire was to achieve them, I would put in place a strategy to overcome them. As early as age nine, for example, I knew I wanted to make money, so I shoveled snow in the winter and mowed lawns in the summer. At twelve, I wanted to learn to swim, so I would swim daily to teach myself. My sister Stephanie would look at me as if I was crazy when I came home with red eyes and tanned skin. She later told me she never had to worry about me because I would go after what I wanted once I set my mind to it. And my competitive mindset led me to play Little League and football throughout high school.

Finding Myself at a Crossroads

After high school, I went on to college at Eastern Kentucky University. While in college, I joined the Marine Corps Reserves. I had always planned to join the reserves, and I felt the time was right. My focus on my education had been slipping because I had started being more social. So, when Dad picked me up from college for winter break, I told him I wanted to join the reserves. He and Mom both asked me why I wanted to do this, and I told them I wanted a challenge. They asked me, what if there's a war? How would I handle it? I told them that obviously I'd have to go. I knew deep inside that I was going in the wrong direction and had to get back on track regardless of what I would face. And then a war did begin, which changed how I view society on many fronts.

My Deployment

During my summer break from college in 1990, I worked at *The Courier-Journal* newspaper. I still attended my monthly Marine Corps Reserve duty training and two-week active-duty training. The active-duty training was generally during the summertime. My supervisor at the newspaper, Thomas, was himself a second lieutenant in the Army Reserves, so he was accommodating to my schedule. I will never forget that day in August of 1990 when Thomas came to me and asked if I had heard that Saddam Hussein had invaded Kuwait. I said, "No," but I immediately felt, in my spirit, that the conflict would affect me. Days later, President George H. W. Bush declared that the U.S. would hold Iraq accountable for invading Kuwait. United States troops and coalition forces began to build up forces in that region. In November 1990, I was activated for the Gulf War and arrived in Saudi Arabia in December 1990.

Being activated was a moment of profound responsibility, a duty I had willingly accepted. It was a decision that not only affected me but also my family. Dad was not a man of much emotion, but when I told him the news, his expression was one of great concern. I then told my mother and the rest of my family, and everyone was upset and worried. My sisters cried, and I did as well, mainly because I did not know if I would live, die, or come back home injured for life. While I was afraid of the unknown, I knew I had to go because I had signed up, which was part of my commitment and who I was as a man.

The week after Thanksgiving, Mom and Dad took me to the formation at Fort Knox, Kentucky, where I was attached to Alpha Company of 8th Tanks. I clearly remember telling them goodbye and thinking it could be the last time I would see them. Alpha Company was attached to H & S Company out of New York. The battalion consisted of several companies that ran up and down the East Coast from New York to Miami, Florida. The entire battalion's first stop was Camp Lejeune, North Carolina, where we prepared to go to the Gulf. This experience taught me the value of family, the importance of commitment, and the necessity of facing our fears head-on.

We arrived at Camp Lejeune a week after Thanksgiving. I had a hollow feeling as I walked into my formation because I knew this was now my reality. The entire division formed as we went through several processing stations and procedures to prepare for our Southeast Asian mission. When we arrived in Saudi Arabia, we continuously moved from location to location for security and strategic reasons. Our living conditions depended on where we were encamped. We slept in tents and, when mobilized, slept wherever possible, in the truck or on the ground. We had daily physical fitness exercises to maintain our stamina. Before the war started, there was a great deal of downtime. We played cards, listened to music, made calls home, and wrote letters. Having downtime was vital, as it took our minds off the current situation and conditions. As we moved closer to the front line, everyone's stress level increased because the risks increased. We were all on edge, even if we did not want to admit it.

I was an enlisted soldier, which meant I had to do a lot of the laborious work and did not agree with all orders. Often, I spoke my mind, whether I felt an order was good or bad. In one instance, I had to do a 14-hour fire watch, which is when soldiers monitor an area for safety. It was a common practice in all branches of service. This fire watch was over a rock mine that dropped hundreds of feet into the earth. The crater stretched for about two miles, and beyond it was the nearest road.

In addition, we did not have any rounds (bullets) in our rifles to protect ourselves and our fellow troops. I did my fire watch as instructed, but I adamantly expressed my frustration about the fire watch the next day. I asked and pressed our platoon leader, "How safe can we be when we do not have any rounds?" He told me that if there was an emergency, we were supposed to run to the Non-Commissioned Officer's tent to inform them. That did not make sense to me, so I pressed the sergeant about it. If a terrorist approached, immediate action would be needed, I said. Thankfully, he listened to me, and rounds were supplied to protect ourselves on future fire watches.

The famous quote, "War is hell," is absolutely true! Being in battle will test your man or womanhood, sanity, and faith in God!

Leading up to liberating Kuwait, I recall at least 30 or more days of constant bombing from our aerial forces. We were on the front line and could feel the effects of the bombs. Often, we would see the bombers flying toward their targets, then, soon after, we would hear the noise and feel the vibrations. We would often shout, "Get some!" to signify that our aerial forces were taking care of business. When the time finally came to move in to liberate Kuwait, everyone was ready to go because of the long wait. We did not know what to expect in this war because Iraq had a large army, and the possibility of becoming a casualty was a real danger. The night before we moved in, we were allowed to make final calls home. Many did, but I decided not to because I depended on my faith to make it through the war. I held on to Hebrews 11:1, the Scripture regarding faith, where it is hoped for but not seen.

Liberating Kuwait

We had to wear our chemical warfare equipment in case of the unexpected with Hussein's regime. The common-sense belief was that if he used chemical warfare against his own people, he would use it against us. Moving into Kuwait occurred over many days and without much resistance. We took mortar fire, but the Iraqis were way off target. When we stopped at night, it was so dark I could not even see my hand in front of my face. The darkness came from the residue of the oil well fires the Hussein regime ignited. So many oil wells were burning, blocking both the sun and the moon from shining. I remember hearing the constant sound of bombings from warplanes and firing artillery. Our unit was so close to the artillery cannons that the concussions from the blast vibrated through our bodies and trucks. Earplugs did very little to soften the sound of the explosions. Luckily, the war was over in a matter of days, and I am very thankful that the strategy was to bomb the Iraqis to soften their fortress and stronghold. It also opened the lanes for the ground forces to push into Kuwait. Upon arrival in Kuwait, the Iraqis had already quit due to starvation, lack of firepower, and as a result of our bombing.

War Shaped Who I Am

My Persian Gulf experience forced me to reflect on my life and who I was. The thought of being home was a dream because I did not know if I would ever see it again. I often thought about my family, friends, and the woman I was dating. I thought about life and the meaning of it. I also thought about my education and where I was going academically. Through reflection and self-awareness, I realized I had to change my life. I decided to transfer from Eastern Kentucky University to the University of Louisville. It was a difficult decision because even though I had grown and developed many relationships at Eastern, it was only one chapter of my life, and now I needed to move to a new chapter.

I also developed a greater appreciation for life and a better awareness of how society operated. I thought about my being in the Gulf War: Was it for idealistic reasons to liberate a country, or was it for other reasons? Countries usually go to war to acquire resources or because resources have been taken from them, and this affects economies. Everything I experienced, witnessed, and absorbed from the war changed my perspective on life and our society.

Discovering Who Am I

Ask yourself, "Who am I?" I invite you to look inside yourself to answer this question. Doing so could bring self-awareness of who you are as a man and what you stand for in life. It is very tempting and very common to see yourself as someone you admire. It's easy to get caught up when we see people in the media or sports world who we want to emulate. For example, Michael Jordan was so great that "I want to be like Mike!" became an entire marketing campaign and today everyone on the planet knows that slogan and the song. Even the great LeBron James said he wanted to be like Michael Jordan. That's why he wears his number. It's fine to look up to people and learn their habits and traits so you can incorporate them into your life, but the reality is that we cannot live as someone else because we all have our own unique personalities, gifts, and talents. Of course, depending on who you are and where you are in life, it can be a challenge to find your purpose, but you must never lose hope. If you truly want to and are willing to work at it, you can get back on the right track and live life fully.

We are all born with a special purpose, and we must recognize and utilize it!

Regardless of your age and where you are in life, I want you to find a place without distractions so you can begin to find the real you through exploration and reflection. Who am I? Maybe it's an easy question and maybe it isn't, but either way, you must be truthful. Consider your authentic self, not your profession, educational credentials, or status. Seek out your core character, behaviors, and abilities. To assist you in this process, sit down in a quiet place with a notebook and a pen and answer the following questions:

1, What are your core values?

- What principles guide your decisions and actions?

- What is essential to you in life?

2. What do you stand for?

- What are your strengths and passions?

- What are you good at?

- What do you enjoy doing?

- What are you passionate about?

- What makes you unique?

3. What are your goals and aspirations?

- What do you want to achieve in life?

- What are your dreams and ambitions?

- What kind of impact do you want to make?

4. What is driving you in life?

- Is your desire to be great driving you?

- Do you want to make more money?

- Are family responsibilities driving you?

5. What are your biggest influences?

- Who has shaped the person you are today?

- What experiences have had the most significant impact on your life?

- What role models do you look up to?

6. What makes you happy and fulfilled?

- What brings you joy?

- Do you get joy out of helping others?

- What are you most grateful for?

- What makes life meaningful to you?

When questioning who we are, we must face both the good and the bad. What do you stand for? Knowing what you want to stand for is important because life will test you in many ways, and knowing who you are will help you stand up for your beliefs without guilt. Being in the Persian Gulf War tested me to my core. War is hell, and the reality is that you have no idea if you're going to come home alive, injured, or in a body bag. The thought of coming home was a dream because I could not imagine it. Being in the war was sobering, and I had to accept that I was not always being the best I could be because I was living life as it came to me instead of being more focused on what was most important. So, I promised myself that if I returned home, I would be more focused on what was important to me.

What's Next After Discovering Who You Are?

As I grew, I often encountered situations that could have distracted me from my goals and kept me from discovering who I was as a man. But I knew I was a man of principle who believed in doing the right thing. I aimed to treat people the way I wanted to be treated, that is, with respect. I discovered my passion as well, which is educating and helping people reach their full potential. I do this in different ways, such as teaching and through my business. No matter what I am doing, I do everything I can to empower people to be the best version of themselves that they can be in life, as parents, in their profession, and as human beings. That is who I am.

Once you discover who you are, your passions and skills will transfer to various areas of your life. For example, as a parent, I empower and teach my children about life and the steps they must take to avoid pitfalls. As a teacher, I discuss life with my students, and talk about some of my experiences, what career moves they should consider making, and what type of relationships they should try to build. As a business owner, I apply my years of experience, education, business successes, and yes, failures, to coaching and crafting strategies for businesses to become more functional and operational.

Discovering who you are is a process that continues throughout life, as you have new experiences and gain knowledge. But what is important is knowing who you are at your core, what drives you, and what your values are. For example, at my core I am still Alan Benson from 30 years ago, but my experiences taught me more about myself and how to handle complex situations. That is not to say that I have completed the journey of discovering who I am because I know that we all evolve over time. To help you develop, redevelop, or sustain who you are, I have created a 90-day plan for discovering and focusing on who you are. This plan is broken down into weekly activities designed to help you find out all you can about yourself. The idea is to encourage reflection, exploration, and action to help you better understand what you are made of—your character, work ethic, talents, social tendencies, preferences, and motivations.

Week 1: Foundations

- Daily Journaling: Each day, find a quiet place to reflect on your day's events, thoughts, and feelings. Be true to yourself and assess what you liked about your day and what you disliked about it. Did you meet anyone of significance? Did you help anyone? Did you find out something new about yourself?

- Personality Exploration: Take an online personality test to gain insights into your strengths and tendencies. Some suggestions are 12 3test.com and bigfive-test.com.

- Values Exercise: Identify core values (e.g., honesty, kindness, loyalty) that resonate with you. What drives you every day, and what do you value?

Week 2: Work Ethic & Habits

- Goal Setting: Set a SMART goal (Specific, Measurable, Achievable, Relevant, Time-bound) for the week and track progress.

- Time Management: Experiment with different time management techniques. There are free apps that can help, such as Todoist and TickTick.

- Mindfulness Practice: Introduce mindfulness into your day through short meditation sessions to increase self-awareness.

Week 3: Talents & Skills

- Skill Inventory: List your skills and talents, from sports to creative pursuits.

- New Skill Exploration: Try a new activity or hobby you've been curious about (e.g., coding, painting, playing a musical instrument, learning a language).

- Strengths & Weaknesses Analysis: Reflect on areas where you excel and areas you'd like to improve.

Week 4: Your Social Connections

- Communication Styles: Learn about different communication styles and practice active listening skills.

- Social Observation: Pay attention to social cues and body language in interactions with others.

- Meaningful Conversations: Engage in deeper conversations with family and friends about values and aspirations.

Week 5: Likes & Dislikes

- "Yes/No" Experiment: Throughout the week, consciously note things you enjoy and things you dislike, from activities to food to music genres.

- Sensory Exploration: Pay close attention to sensory experiences (e.g., favorite scents, textures, sounds) to identify your preferences.

- "Ideal Day" Visualization: Imagine and describe your perfect day in detail.

Week 6: Drive & Purpose

- Role Models: Identify individuals you admire and analyze the qualities that inspire you.

- "Why" Questions: To uncover your underlying motivations, ask yourself "why" you do certain things.

- Vision Board: Create a visual representation of your goals, dreams, and aspirations.

Week 7: Putting It All Together

- Self-Reflection: Review your journal entries from the past weeks to identify patterns and insights.

- Action Plan: Based on self-discovery of who you are, create a plan for pursuing interests, improving skills, and building meaningful connections.

- Sharing & Feedback: Share what you discovered with a trusted friend or mentor and ask them for feedback and support.

- Putting your plan into action: Execute your plan and watch as it helps you grow!

Weeks 8-12: Exploration & Experimentation

- Continue Journaling: Maintain consistent journaling practice to track progress and reflect on experiences.

- Skill Development: Dedicate weekly time to developing chosen skills or pursuing new interests.

- Social Exploration: Attend social events, join clubs, or volunteer so you can meet new people and expand your social circle.

- Challenge Comfort Zones: Step outside your comfort zone by trying new things and facing fears.

Important Considerations:

- Individualization: Adapt this plan to your own pace and interests.

- Support System: Seek out a supportive network of friends, family, and/or mentors.

- Open-Mindedness: Remember, self-discovery is an ongoing journey, and changing and evolving is okay.

- Celebrate Successes: Self-reflection is important, and so is acknowledging your progress.

My path to discovering who I am as a man has been eye-opening and ongoing, shaped by many experiences and challenges. From my childhood curiosity and early mishaps, like when I narrowly escaped electrocution, to the impact of the Persian Gulf War, my experiences have not only revealed my core values and passions but have also fueled my desire to empower others to reach their full potential.

The Persian Gulf War transformed my life. It forced me to confront my fears, question my purpose, and, ultimately, redefine who I was. It was a sobering experience that made me appreciate the fragility of life and the importance of living with intentionality.

Upon returning home, I felt a renewed purpose and a deep desire to get Alan back on track. This led me to pursue my passion for education and helping others. Whether through teaching, business coaching, or simply being a supportive presence in the lives of those around me, I strive to empower others to be their best selves.

My experiences have taught me that who I am is not a destination but an ongoing journey. As I continue to evolve, I remain committed to embracing new challenges, learning, and living a life that aligns with my authentic self.

The 90-day self-discovery plan outlined in this chapter is a testament to my belief in the power of reflection and deliberate action. My wish is that it will serve as a guide for you as you embark on your own journey of self-discovery. Discovering who you are is well worth the effort and time and even the occasional pain it may bring, because it will also bring you enlightenment.

Chapter 3: Taming Distractions

Silencing the Noise

In high school, I dreamed of being a star football player and track star, and the only way to get to the point of stardom was to focus and put in the work. While that was many years ago, putting in the work and concentrating on doing it was most important. To focus, I kept out the noise, which was not an easy task to accomplish. Today, noise comes to us from so many directions. Both internal and external, this constant barrage can be a significant obstacle to focus, productivity, and overall well-being. There's the internal noise—the ceaseless stream of thoughts, worries, and self-doubt that repeats itself in our minds. This mental noise can range from replaying past conversations in our head to worrying about future tasks, and it keeps us from fully engaging in the present moment. Then there are external distractions that add another layer of disruption. The constant buzz of notifications, the enticements of social media, and the sheer volume of information bombarding us every day can distract us from what truly matters. Finally, there is the constant busyness that defines our lives. Our often-packed schedules leave little room for quiet reflection or concentrated focus.

All this internal and external noise can make us feel overwhelmed and scattered. It can diminish our ability to be present, stifle creativity, and ultimately lead to a sense of dissatisfaction. By recognizing and understanding these different types of noise, you can find ways to silence them and cultivate focus and discipline.

Why Is Silencing the Noise Important to Growing in Life?

When I speak of noise, I am speaking of what we can physically hear as well as what we hear in our head. Noise can come from all kinds of directions and situations. It can play on our emotions and self-confidence. For example, I was laid off from a job while married. As a man, that devastated me because I was the breadwinner. I had to demonstrate confidence to my wife that we would be okay because I did not want her to become overly worried, but deep inside, I was afraid of the unknown. I could not show that to her. One thing I knew I had to do was find employment quickly. But I also knew that would be a short-term fix, so while working the job I *had* to work, I continued to look for the job I *wanted*. I even worked a second job. Doing what you have to do can be a weight on your shoulders, but you have to be strong-willed, have faith, and network in order to get where you want to be. You also have to condition your mind to remember that this will only be temporary.

Your willpower and confidence will be tested in many situations; sometimes, we cannot explain why these situations occur. Nevertheless, it is wise to do a self-inventory to try to determine how it happened, why it happened, if you contributed to it happening, or if it was beyond your control. Answering those questions will allow you to determine if any external factors contributed to the situation or if your actions played a role. Life will throw both rewards and disappointments at you. We all fall, but do you fall on your face or on your back? If you fall on your face, you cannot see what is happening around you. But if you fall on your back, you can see all around you and make better decisions next time. Some hardships we go through are self-inflicted, while others are beyond our control. How you handle it is the key to overcoming it, and knowing how to silence the noise is essential to learning more about yourself, growing up and implementing a plan to correct the "why."

On the other hand, not understanding or correcting the "why" could tear you down or lead you to run in circles. I know we all are built differently and are affected by situations differently. For example, on numerous occasions, I have seen people turn to alcohol when they're going through a problem. I have also seen people turn to more positive ways of handling situations. I have been on both sides, and I can tell you that drinking only offers a short-term state of forgetfulness, but it ultimately puts you in a bottomless pit of despair. A positive approach to tame the internal and external noise is the best way to conquer any negative situation in which you find yourself.

Taming the Noise

As we travel through life, there will be times when we must tame the noise. How we tame it is essential to our mental and physical well-being. There are ways to do it. Each could clear your mind, calm any fears, and give you ideas for moving forward. Below are some proven strategies for taming the noise that distracts us from our goals.

1. Meditation: Meditation is a powerful tool for managing internal noise and focuses on bringing awareness to the situation. Techniques like concentrating on your breathing or body sensations help train your mind to recognize and observe intrusive thoughts without getting caught up in them. Over time, with regular practice, you can gently redirect the internal dialogue, promoting greater focus.

2. Listening to Music: Music can distract you from your current situation and calm your mind and spirit. This could be part of your meditation process.

3. Exercising: Exercising relieves stress and clears the mind. It is an excellent way to regain perspective of a situation and opens your mind to developing solutions. Riding your bike, taking a nature walk, lifting weights, or jogging are just a few of the many ways to tame the noise.

4. Journaling: Constant mental chatter often stems from unresolved anxieties or worries. Journaling provides an outlet for expressing these thoughts and emotions on paper. By externalizing them, you can gain clarity and perspective, so you can let go of the mental burden and focus on the present task.

Embracing Silence to Tame the Noise

Our world is filled with notifications, music, and the general hum of activity; silence can feel like a luxury. We are constantly moving and busy. We sometimes have our earbuds in, listening to music, a podcast, or whatever else the world has to offer. Most of us rarely have or take the time to embrace being quiet. Embracing quiet moments benefits our mental, emotional, and even physical well-being. There is nothing like being in a quiet place and space. You can think, breathe calmly, and relax. My quiet spaces are the library, riding my bike alone, or walking down a peaceful nature trail. Below are some benefits to carving out space for silence:

1. A Refuge from Stress: Our modern lives are filled with stressors, and constant noise can heighten this tension. Silence acts as a sanctuary.

2. A Gateway to Self-Awareness: The constant noise of the external world can drown out our inner voice. Silence allows us to turn inward, quieting the mental noise and opening the door for greater reflection. We can observe our thoughts and feelings without judgment, gaining

a deeper understanding of ourselves.[1] This self-awareness can be crucial for emotional regulation and managing challenges with enhanced clarity.

3. A Spark for Creativity: Though some may think of silence as the absence of thought, it is, in fact, an opportunity for creative ideas to germinate. When our minds are not bombarded with external stimuli, they are able to wander, make meaningful connections, and find inspiration. Artists, writers, and problem solvers have long recognized the power of silence to unlock their creative potential.

4. A Boost for Focus and Productivity: In a world obsessed with multitasking, silence can be a powerful tool for enhancing focus. Without distractions, we can concentrate more deeply on a task, increasing efficiency and productivity. Whether working on a complex project or simply trying to be present in a conversation, embracing quiet allows us to give our full attention to what truly matters.

5. A Deeper Connection with Ourselves and the World: Silence allows us to appreciate the subtle beauty of the world around us. We can become more attuned to the sounds of nature, the rhythm of our own breathing, and the simple underlying hum of existence. This heightened awareness fosters a deeper connection between us and the environment, promoting peace and belonging.

Remember, consistency is key. Incorporating these small pockets of silence into your daily routine will cultivate peace and clarity that will benefit every aspect of your life. You are also developing discipline by taking control of the internal and external noise around you. The more you practice silence, the more you build discipline for positioning yourself to seek and achieve what you wish for in life.

---

1. Barboza, "Approaching Stress with Curiosity."

Finding Your Focus to Tame the Noise

One day, I was talking to my late fraternity brother, Mark Mitchell, and he asked how my kids were doing. I said they were doing well and told him that I had taught them to maintain their focus. He said, "Alan, you sound just like my father." He explained that he would go to his father with his problems, and his father would advise him to remain focused. This is sound advice because focus turns our attention to what needs to be done. It pushes out anything that might not be as relevant or need attention at that moment. We can lose our focus for any number of reasons, including not knowing how to prioritize life's matters. But focus closes the door on unwanted noise, so it's crucial to have the ability to sustain it. Below are some proven benefits to maintaining focus.

The Benefits of Being Focused

1. Helps Achieve Goals: Focus gives us the discipline to achieve our goals. It allows us to break down significant goals into smaller, manageable tasks, making them less overwhelming and more attainable.

2. Promotes Completion of Tasks: Focus allows us to tune out distractions and concentrate on the work at hand. It improves the quality of our work and enables us to complete tasks more efficiently.

3. Minimizes Procrastination: Focus gives us the willpower to resist putting things off. It makes us more productive and reduces stress caused by looming deadlines.

4. Improves Time Management: Focus helps us prioritize tasks and manage time more effectively. This means we can do more in less time, which leaves us with more free time for leisure activities.

5. Cultivates Healthier Habits: Focus is essential for forming and sticking to healthy habits, like regular exercise, healthy eating, and getting enough sleep. It pushes us to exercise even when we do not feel like it. This contributes to overall well-being and a better quality of life.

6. Bolsters Mental Resilience: Focus strengthens our ability to cope with challenges and setbacks. It helps us persevere through difficult times and bounce back from failures.

7. Sharpens Decision-Making: Focus allows us to make well-considered decisions by ensuring that we carefully weigh our options and avoid impulsive choices.

8. Encourages Self-Reliance: Focus fosters self-reliance by reminding us to take responsibility for our actions, as well as our accomplishments.

9. Builds Enduring Confidence: Focus leads to confidence, which grows as we achieve our goals. We start to believe in our abilities and take on more significant challenges.

10. Fosters Consistent Performance: Focus helps us maintain a consistent level of performance in all areas of life. Employers, colleagues, and friends value this reliability.

As you probably already know, life has many twists and turns, and the older we get, the more responsibilities we have. If you're a teen or an adolescent, for example, you know you'll eventually need transportation and a place to live. Responsibilities also come with being in a relationship, and even more with being married. I recall my father explaining to me that getting married comes with certain responsibilities and how one needs to be prepared for them. And if children enter the equation, the responsibilities multiply. Such responsibilities can distract you or cause you to shift your focus to the back burner because you must deal with matters that need your immediate attention. My point is that we must consider the cost of taking on additional responsibilities and make sure to have a plan to manage them while maintaining focus.

For instance, I was in school when my then-wife and I had twins. We agreed that I would continue my schooling after they were born. I also shared the workload of raising them, especially because they were twins. I played an active role in feeding them every morning, and during the first seven months, one wanted to eat at 2 a.m. and 5 a.m. every morning. I also helped dress them and take them to daycare, since it was down the street from where I worked. Was it exhausting? Extremely. I often went to class with only two hours of sleep, but I knew they would eventually start sleeping through the night, and I was determined to finish school.

The level of support we have or don't have can also throw off our focus. Some people do not have family or any other support at all, and this is likely to compound their struggles and affect their decisions. During my divorce, I attended a conference and interviewed with a company that was impressed with my credentials and wanted me to be a plant manager at one of their plants in California. But it was over 2000 miles from my home, and I would be far from my kids. I refused to be the type of man who only sees his kids occasionally. I was determined to play an active role in their lives, so I lost interest in that job. Even though I was focused on landing a career job, I knew I had to ensure it would be close to where I lived because of my family responsibilities.

Whether you have to shift focus, put it on the back burner or are finally trying to find it, it is never too late to re-focus or to become focused. Below are strategies that will help you find your focus or get back to being focused.

How to Find Your Focus

1. Define Your "Why": Concentrate on what needs to be completed and then complete it. This "why" will be your fuel when you encounter obstacles or distractions.

2. Schedule It: Treat your commitments to yourself as respectfully as you would a business meeting. Block out dedicated time in your calendar for focusing work on your goal.

3. Craft Your Environment: Minimize distractions by creating a space conducive to focus. Silence notifications, tidy your workspace, and use

tools that block distracting websites or apps.

4. Make Routine Your Friend: Consistency is key. The more you stick to your schedule, the easier it will be to follow through and make discipline a habit.

5. Find an Accountability Partner: Share your goals with a friend, colleague, or online community. Knowing someone is checking in can provide extra motivation and support.

6. Celebrate Small Wins: Acknowledge and reward yourself for reaching milestones, no matter how small. This positive reinforcement helps you stay motivated.

7. Embrace Setbacks: Everyone slips up sometimes. Don't beat yourself up—think of setbacks as learning opportunities. Analyze what went wrong and adjust your approach for the next time.

8. Prioritize Self-Care: You can't pour from an empty cup. Ensure you sleep well, eat healthy foods, and take breaks to avoid burnout. A healthy body and mind are fundamental for sustained discipline.

9. Focus on Progress, Not Perfection: Discipline is a journey, not a destination. There will be bumps along the road. The goal is to keep moving forward and celebrate your overall progress.

How to Get Back to Being Focused

1. Revisit Your "Why": Sometimes motivation gets lost in the shuffle. Remind yourself of the reasons behind your goals. Why did you want to be disciplined in the first place? Reconnecting with that purpose can reignite your passion.

2. Identify Triggers: What throws you off track? Is it social media? Lack of sleep? Pinpointing your triggers allows you to develop strategies to

avoid them or create buffers.

3. Audit Your Schedule: Be honest about how you're spending your time. Are there hidden time sucks? Revamp your schedule to prioritize your goals and eliminate unnecessary distractions.

4. Start Fresh with Small Wins: Don't jump back into overwhelming challenges. Pick a small, achievable goal to get back on track. The feeling of accomplishment will boost your confidence and motivation.

5. Rework Your Environment: Focusing is more challenging when your surroundings are chaotic or filled with temptations. Revamp your workspace or create routines that minimize distractions.

6. Reconnect with Your Accountability Partner: Chat with your accountability partner. Reiterate your goals and seek their support. Having someone to check in with can provide a much-needed boost.

7. Forgive Yourself and Move On: Dwelling on past slip-ups will only further derail you. Acknowledge the setback, learn from it, and recommit to your goals.

8. Reward Progress, Not Perfection: Focus on celebrating your steps forward, no matter how small. This positive reinforcement keeps you motivated on the path to discipline.

9. Reassess Your Goals: Have your priorities or circumstances changed? It's okay to adjust your goals as needed. Just take care to make sure they still align with your current aspirations.

10. Find Inspiration: Read success stories, listen to motivational podcasts, or surround yourself with positive people. External inspiration can help you refocus and rekindle your commitment to discipline.

Chapter 4: Beyond the Surface

Developing Character

We're all born with personality traits that define who we are. These traits are linked to our bloodline from our parents and can go back generations. For example, I share certain personality traits with my father, such as being reserved and somewhat introverted. But this doesn't mean either of us is shy; we engage with people and speak up when we feel the need. How we are raised also shapes the exposure we receive and influences the habits and beliefs we develop.

As you move down the road of life, there will be times when you must make decisions that test your character as a man. These decisions could be financial or personal, like those involving relationships. Regardless of the situation, you will be tested, and the truth is that there will be times when you make the wrong choice. We all have, and that is part of life. For instance, when I taught an ethics class, the first thing I asked the students was if they had seen me walking into class and dropping a $100 bill, how many of them would tell me? Only a couple of students raised their hands. One student even said it would be my loss!

When we are taught how to handle various situations, making some decisions can be easier. For example, I learned early on not to drink or do drugs because they can destroy your life. I understood that, so even though I occasionally drink today, I do so responsibly. If I feel I've had too much, I will ask someone else to drive. But what if you are not taught how to behave responsibly? What are the right decisions to make, who can you turn to for answers, and how do you know you are making the right choice? If you find yourself asking these questions, remember that there are ways we should behave based on our fundamental understanding of right and wrong, and following through with what is right or wrong will depend heavily on your character.

What Is Character?

Character is the collection of qualities that define your moral and ethical nature. It includes honesty, integrity, courage, kindness, and respect. These traits make you a dependable, trustworthy, and admirable person. Character serves as the foundation for building strong relationships, successful careers, and meaningful lives. When you think about character, what comes to mind? Do you reflect on who you are, your qualities, values, and actions? Having character is what makes someone an upstanding person. It is the core that determines whether you're a good friend, a dependable teammate, and a responsible citizen.

Character is like the engine of a car. A car with a strong engine can go anywhere, handle any terrain, and last for years. Similarly, a person with strong character can overcome challenges, make tough decisions, perform under pressure, and ultimately lead a fulfilling life. Character isn't something you're born with; it's something you build over time, brick by brick. It's like a muscle that becomes stronger with exercise: the more you work on it, the stronger it becomes. We begin building character by being aware of our actions and following through on them. If, for example, you tell someone you will do something, you keep your word. It's about standing tall with a mindset of treating others as you would like to be treated. Here are a few tips:

1. Know your values: What do you stand for? What's important to you? Identify your core beliefs and then live by them.

2. Tell the truth: Honesty is the foundation of trust. Act with integrity, even when it's hard.

3. Own your mistakes: Accept responsibility for your actions and honor your promises.

4. Show respect: Treat others with kindness and respect, even if they don't deserve it.

5. Act with kindness: Kindness can go a long way. Do something nice for someone without having an agenda.

6. Cultivate patience: Good things take time. Don't expect instant results.

7. Be persistent: Keep your eye on your goals. Work hard and smart.

8. Stay focused: Direct your energies toward your goals and ignore the noise around you.

9. Express gratitude: Appreciate the good things in your life.

10. Practice humility: Avoid bragging or boasting. Let your actions speak for themselves.

11. Become a good listener: Pay attention to what others say.

12. Develop strong communication: Express yourself clearly and effec-

tively.

13. Become a good problem-solver: Don't let problems overwhelm you. Break them down into smaller steps and tackle them one at a time.

14. Evolve into a good decision-maker: Think carefully before you act. Consider all your options and choose the best course of action.

15. Serve as a positive role model: Set a good example for others.

16. Become a lifelong learner: Never stop learning and growing.

17. Transform your failures into opportunities: Failure is not a time to stop; it is a time to learn so you can climb to higher ground.

18. Embrace practical wisdom: Learn to listen attentively, ask what-ifs, and explore the costs and benefits of different paths.

19. Have faith: Always think positively by praying and believing.

20. Believe in yourself: There is only one you. Believe in your abilities and have confidence.

Building a strong character takes time and effort because it requires discipline and practice. It is like building strength and stamina to run a 400-meter dash. It takes time, effort, and consistent practice. You can't expect to become a strong, ethical person overnight. You need discipline, patience, and a willingness to learn and grow. Think of it this way: every time you choose to be honest, even when it's tough, you're strengthening your character muscle. Every time you resist temptation, you're building your self-control. Every time you help someone in need, you're developing your empathy. Just as you wouldn't expect to become a skilled athlete without regular training, you can't expect to develop a strong character without consistent effort. It's about making conscious choices, even when it's not easy, and holding yourself accountable as you strive to be your best self. It comes down to knowing the difference between right and wrong, and acting on that knowledge.

Knowing the Difference Between Right and Wrong

Personally, I am always looking for challenges and ways to overcome them. Thinking this way has its benefits and its drawbacks. For instance, when I was 11, I wanted to make money. Did I go out and steal it? Of course not! I shoveled snow in the winter and mowed lawns in the summer. The drawback of seeking out challenges to overcome was that my curiosity sometimes got me into trouble, like when my mother told me not to go down to the river, but I went anyway, and I sunk into a mud hole up to my waist! But let's return to my efforts to earn some money. Why did I shovel snow instead of finding illegal ways to get it, like stealing? For starters, I knew there would be serious and painful consequences from my parents. More importantly, I was taught in church not to steal. I realize we are all raised in different households and under different circumstances, some more difficult than others, but I also know there are resources available for those in need, so stealing should never be acceptable.

If you are unsure about what is right and wrong, below is a list, along with explanations, for your consideration.

The right things:

- Respect: Show kindness and respect to everyone, regardless of their background or beliefs.

- Honesty: Always tell the truth. It fosters trust and helps you maintain integrity.

- Responsibility: Take ownership of your actions and their consequences.

- Kindness: Even small acts of kindness can significantly improve someone's day.

- Empathy: Aim to understand others' feelings and imagine yourself in their position.

- Gratitude: Appreciate what you have, both big and small.

- Hard Work: Dedicate effort to your studies, work, and hobbies.

- Perseverance: Keep going when things get tough. Continue trying your best.

- Learn: Stay open to learning new things and developing as an individual.

- Help Others: Offer assistance to those in need.

- Keep Promises: Follow through on what you commit to.

- Be Punctual: Respect others' time by arriving on time.

- Take Care of Yourself: Eat healthy, exercise, and get enough sleep.

- Appreciate Nature: Take time to connect with the natural world.

- Embrace Your Creativity: Pursue your artistic passions, no matter what they are.

- Set Goals: Set high standards and actively pursue your dreams.

- Save Money: Learn to save for the future and for a rainy day because life will bring you both good and bad days.

- Practice patience: Remember, good things take time.

- Forgive: Let go of anger and resentment.

- Be Positive: A positive attitude can make an enormous difference.

The wrong things:

- Bullying: Hurting others, either physically or emotionally, is never okay.

- Stealing: Taking things that don't belong to you is wrong.

- Lying: Dishonesty can damage relationships and your reputation.

- Cheating: Taking shortcuts or unfair advantages is not the right way to succeed.

- Being Rude: Speaking harshly or disrespectfully to others is hurtful.

- Giving Up: Quitting when things get tough is a missed opportunity.

- Ignoring Your Health: Neglecting your physical and mental well-being is harmful.

- Being Lazy: Procrastination and laziness will lead you nowhere.

- Judging Others: Everyone makes mistakes. Don't be quick to judge.

- Being Selfish: Think about others' needs and feelings.

- Wasting Time: Use your time wisely and productively.

- Being Negative: A negative attitude can bring down everyone around you, including yourself.

- Disrespecting Authority: Follow rules and respect those in positions of authority.

- Using Harmful Substances: Drugs and alcohol can have serious consequences.

- Cyberbullying: Bullying others online is just as harmful as bullying in person.

- Spreading Rumors: Gossip can hurt people's feelings and make people angry.

- Being Envious: Be happy for others' successes.

- Being Fearful: Face your fears and take risks.

- Ignoring Your Responsibilities: Take care of your duties and commitments.

- Being Unappreciative: Be thankful for the good things in your life.

Knowing and doing what's right will help you shape the person you want to be and the world you want to live in. When you choose the right path, you're building a foundation of integrity, respect, and empathy. This foundation will support you through life's hurdles and help you reach your full potential. On the other hand, choosing the wrong path can have serious consequences. Dishonesty, for example, can damage your reputation and erode others' trust in you. It can lead to isolation and missed opportunities. Similarly, disrespecting others can harm relationships and create conflict. It can also cause feelings of guilt and shame.

Making the right choices can lead to a fulfilling and rewarding life. It can help you build strong relationships, achieve your goals, and positively impact the world. So, the next time you're faced with a decision, take a moment to consider the consequences of your actions. Choose wisely, young man. Your future depends on it.

Having Character Matters!

I remember my time in the Marine Corps like it was yesterday. In boot camp, the drill instructors would shout that it built character for every problematic task we had to complete as recruits. Whether going down the slide for life, being in the gas chamber, rappelling, or low crawling on my elbows and knees while ordnances went off above my head, that constant calling was always shouted: "It builds character!!" I didn't yet understand how it built character, but as I grew and faced various challenges, I began to understand. I have learned that we all face challenges that test our willpower, integrity, and identity. Being in the Marines prepared me to keep my head up while facing difficult situations. It taught me how to think under pressure and to think systematically. The Marines, as well as my upbringing, were both instrumental in shaping my character. I was taught always to do the right thing, treat people how I wanted to be treated, be honest, work hard, and hold my head high.

I feel grateful for the life experiences that helped shape me into the man I am today. I am not claiming that I have arrived because life is a continuous process of adjusting, reflecting, and sometimes making pivots to move forward. However, at my core as a man, my character speaks and shows others what I stand for; that is why having an upright and strong character is crucial to me. Character gives me the strength to get back up when I fall. And when you know what is right, you can stand by it and hold your head high with dignity, even if others doubt you.

I wrote this book to help you develop your character because it will define you as a person, man, husband, and father. So now you might be asking, "Where do I start?" Let's start by better understanding what character is and how to incorporate it into your life.

30-Day Character Development Plan

Character is about actively pursuing good behavior, as well as avoiding bad behavior. It involves living a life of integrity, compassion, and purpose. Practicing these virtues daily helps build a strong character that can only benefit you and those around you. Character development is a process, though; it involves developing certain habits, increasing self-awareness, understanding emotional intelligence, building resilience, and setting goals. Below is a more in-depth description of these concepts, followed by a 30-day plan you can implement to help you build character.

1. Habit Formation:

   ○ Consistency Is Key: Build new positive habits, like mindfulness, gratitude, and empathy.

   ○ Long-term Benefits: These habits can become deeply embedded in your daily routine, resulting in lasting positive changes.

2. Self-Awareness:

   ○ Inner Exploration: Explore your thoughts, feelings, and behaviors.

   ○ Personal Growth: Knowing yourself better helps you make smarter choices and handle situations more effectively.

3. Emotional Intelligence:

   ○ Empathy Development: Empathy helps us connect more deeply with others.

   ○ Stronger Relationships: Improving emotional intelligence fosters healthier and more satisfying relationships.

4. Resilience Building:

   ○ Overcoming Challenges: Resilience is strengthened when we encounter obstacles and practice perseverance.

   ○ Adaptability: Being able to adjust and recover from setbacks is central to resilience.

5. Goal-Setting and Achievement:

   ○ Focused Progress: Set clear goals and monitor your progress.

- ○ Motivation and Drive: Accomplishing small goals builds confidence and encourages us to pursue larger ones.

Again, character development is a lifelong process, but a 30-day plan is an effective starting point. By consistently working on yourself, you can become a better version of yourself and positively influence the world. It isn't always easy, but it's always worth it. Following these steps will help you develop qualities that will lead you to becoming successful and happy. As you embark on this journey, consider writing down your answers and thoughts in a journal.

Week 1: Self-Awareness

- Day 1-5: Identify your core values. What principles guide your life?

- Day 6-10: Reflect on your strengths and weaknesses. What are you naturally good at? What areas could you improve?

Week 2: Mindfulness and Gratitude

- Day 11-15: Practice daily meditation or mindfulness exercises. Focus on your breath and the present moment.

- Day 16-20: Keep a gratitude journal, in which you write down three things you're grateful for each day.

Week 3: Empathy and Kindness

- Day 21-25: Volunteer your time to help others. This could be at a local shelter, food bank, animal shelter, hospital or any organization looking for volunteers.

- Day 26-30: Practice active listening. When someone is speaking, give them your full attention.

Week 4: Perseverance and Goal Setting

- Day 31: Set a specific, achievable goal, and then break it down into smaller steps.

- Day 32-35: Track your progress towards your goal. Celebrate your achievements, no matter how small.

Additional Tips:

- Read books: Choose books that inspire and teach valuable lessons.

- Learn from role models: Identify people who embody the character traits you admire.

- Practice self-discipline: Delay gratification and resist temptations.

- Seek feedback: Ask trusted friends and family for honest feedback on your behavior.

- Embrace challenges: Think of challenges as opportunities for growth.

- Remember, character development is a lifelong process. Be patient with yourself and don't forget to celebrate your progress, however small.

I think it's important to repeat that character is the engine that drives us toward a fulfilling life. It is a door opener and guide for making wise decisions to become the best man you can be. That doesn't mean you'll get everything right all the time. You will make mistakes, face setbacks, and experience disappointments, as we all do. But with a solid character, you will better handle almost any challenge because you will find the strength to stand tall during storms. With stamina and intestinal fortitude, achieving your dreams becomes more accessible and attainable. The sooner you begin working on being the best you can be, the sooner you can start down the path to greatness!

Chapter 5: Discipline
The Key to Unlocking Your Potential

Have you ever dreamed of achieving great things? Deep down, we all long for a hero's journey—a story where we rise from ordinary to extraordinary. We all have the ability to be extraordinary, and often, especially when we're young, we think of doing something remarkable that will attract national or global attention. But you don't need the eyes of the world on you to do great things. For example, you could be a social worker who changes the lives of countless people, many of whom then go on to have stable lives and do good things themselves, and pay it forward, creating a snowball effect of greatness. Now that's impact!

In other words, it's entirely possible to be great without being a public figure recognized by millions. This is a role often called the sidekick. A sidekick is someone closely connected to someone in the limelight, but who isn't necessarily in the limelight themselves. When I think of sidekicks, I think of Drew Bundini Brown, for example. He was the assistant trainer to the G.O.A.T., Muhammad Ali. Not only was he his assistant trainer, but Bundini Brown was also Ali's hype man, writing some of his speeches and poems, including the words Ali became known for, "Float like a butterfly, sting like a bee." Granted, Muhammad Ali is the hero in this scenario, but you don't need to be a superstar, or someone widely recognized, to be a hero.

The truth is, everyday heroes are all around us, including my father, Sam Benson. He was born in Pulaski, Tennessee, but after finishing high school, he moved to Louisville, Kentucky, where he started working at Kosair Children's Hospital as a custodian. Later, he became a brace technician (a medical support professional who fabricates, applies, and removes orthopedic devices for patients), then the manager of the brace shop, and eventually the director. Dad had a 40-year career and, after various mergers and acquisitions that resulted in the renaming of Kosair, retired from Norton's Hospital. While his career progression is impressive, he is my hero because all of my needs and some of my wants were met under his care. He was at every football game I played and was always there for his family. Dad's career ascension was impressive, starting out as a custodian and retiring as a Director of Orthotics and Prosthetics. However, even if Dad had been a custodian for 40 years, who he was in his actions as a man and a father makes him my hero. He was honorable, driven, disciplined, and a firm disciplinarian. There were rules and expectations in his house. The discipline and the work ethic I learned from him carried over into sports and life.

When I was in high school, I ran track, running the 100, 200, and 400-meter sprints during my freshman year. My best event was the 400 meters because I was strong and had endurance and speed. The 400 meters was a sprint, but it was also a strategic race—if you burst out of the blocks like you were running the 100 or 200, you would be exhausted by the 300-meter mark and ultimately lose the race. So even though I had to sprint, I also had to conserve energy for the 300-meter stretch. The 300-meter mark was extremely important because, as my track coach, Chico, would say, that was when "that bear jumps on your back." At that point, I needed mental toughness and strength to push through the rest of the race. This was a learning process during my freshman year; I was learning the techniques and the discipline needed to successfully run track. I competed during my sophomore year but felt I still hadn't quite made my mark as one of the top sprinters at my school.

Now, as I mentioned in the Introduction, there was a track event called "The Meet of Champions," at which all the best runners in Louisville, Kentucky, gathered to compete. I dreamed throughout my sophomore year of competing in that meet because I wanted to be and race with the best in the city. In the offseason, I worked hard to become stronger and faster to improve my performance. I ran stairs, lifted weights, ran long distances, and sprinted to improve. During my summer training, I suffered a setback when I pulled my hamstring. I tried to work through it, but the injury persisted, even during football season. I knew I needed to rest my hamstring because I was only making it worse, so after football season, I rested until track season began.

When track season started, I had healed from my injury and was faster and even more determined, and qualified for "The Meet of Champions." I was excited because I was considered one of the best runners in the 400-meter dash. It was an achievement, and I felt proud of it. Participating in "The Meet of Champions" was one of many goals I have reached in life. It's meaningful because, while I wasn't always aware of it, I was creating a routine that paved my path forward. That path was not only paved with good intentions; it needed the crucial element of discipline.

Why We Crave Discipline: The Hero Within

Imagine a world where every desire is fulfilled, and goals are reached effortlessly. While it sounds appealing, a life lacking discipline lacks direction and meaning. Discipline is the inner strength and motivation that helps us turn dreams into reality. It's the hero inside us, the force that keeps us moving forward even when times are tough. I believe that deep down, we all crave discipline. This might seem counterintuitive. Maybe you see discipline as a restriction, stopping us from receiving instant gratification. But the truth is, discipline is the key that unlocks our true potential, the inner hero eager to emerge. When I played sports, I knew I wanted to start in football and be a champion in track—and I understood that to reach my goals, I had to train in the weight room and run to boost my performance. I did those things because I had discipline.

We all have potential, dreams, and aspirations, but without discipline, they are only desires. We crave that great version of ourselves—the successful rapper, the confident athlete, the well-rounded person. All require discipline. For example, that conscious spirit that wakes you up early to hit the gym and pushes you to keep practicing helps you chip away at distractions, procrastination, and self-doubt, all of which hold you back from becoming your best. Living in a household with rules and participating in sports set the stage for me to develop discipline, as I was young and still learning about myself. Additionally, later experiences, like joining the Marines and completing graduate studies, required discipline. Discipline helped shape me into who I am today because it tested my will and resilience even when I didn't feel like doing the task in front of me.

Why does this craving for discipline exist? Here are some reasons:

- The Hero's Journey Within: Stories of heroes connect with us because they tap into our deep desire for growth and achievement. The hero faces challenges, overcomes obstacles, and emerges stronger. No matter our age or background, we all have a hero's journey inside us. Mine was when I worked hard in the weight room during the offseason of football freshman year and, through my effort, earned a starting spot in my sophomore season.

- The Power of Delayed Gratification: Discipline helps us focus on long-term goals rather than short-term pleasures. We desire the satisfaction of achievement, the feeling that we have worked hard and grown. My desire was to earn a Master of Business Administration (MBA) once I'd earned my undergraduate degree. I understood it would take additional effort and time, but I wanted that degree and I achieved it. Can you think of something you wanted that also required some delayed gratification?

- Building Self-Trust and Confidence: When consistently demonstrating discipline, we build trust in ourselves. We understand that when we set our minds to something, we can achieve it. This self-trust boosts our confidence and encourages us to take on even bigger challenges. With each successful chisel blow, the sculptor becomes more confident in their ability to finish the masterpiece. When I was twelve, I wanted to learn how to swim, so every day, I went to the pool to teach myself until I could swim. This simple action strengthened my self-trust and confidence in myself.

- Creating Structure and Freedom: You may think that discipline seems limiting, but in fact, it offers freedom from the stress of indecision. By establishing routines and boundaries, we bring order to our lives. This order helps us concentrate our energy and relieves us from the mental fatigue of constantly deciding what to do next. Think of an archer who trains hard to perfect their form and technique. Their discipline enables them to focus and hit their target during competition.

Of course, the road to consistent discipline has many obstacles. There will be days when the couch or scrolling through social media seems far more inviting than the gym. I was taught discipline because I had tasks to do as a teenager. I had to wash dishes, clean the walls, take out the garbage, and mow the lawn. That was what was expected of me. Did I like doing the chores? No, but I had to do them, and the lesson was that sometimes we must do things we don't want to do. It's a lesson that applies to my life even today.

When we follow through on tasks we might not want to do, work hard to achieve a goal, and overcome challenges, the hero within truly emerges. We develop the inner strength to silence distractions and commit ourselves to our goals.

Here are some tips to nurture your inner hero and cultivate discipline:

- Start Small: Don't overwhelm yourself with drastic changes. Begin with small, achievable goals and gradually increase the difficulty. Take micro-steps. For example, if you wish to get into shape, don't start with trying to run ten miles; instead, start with one or two miles. Don't forget to celebrate your victories, no matter how small, as this will reinforce positive behavior.

- Find Your "Why": Connect your discipline to a deeper purpose. What are you striving for? A clear "why" will fuel your motivation, especially on tough days. For example, I rode 65 miles in the "Bike to Beat Cancer" event for my mother, who died of stomach cancer in 2016. Why did I do it? I did it to honor my mother and raise money to fight cancer.

- Embrace the Journey: Discipline isn't about perfection; it's about consistent effort. There will be setbacks, but see them as learning opportunities, not failures. The hero's journey is rarely smooth sailing, but the hero keeps going. We all encounter setbacks and curveballs; the key is to never give up.

By embracing discipline, you activate the hero within, the part of us that longs for growth and achievement. With focused effort, we can chip away at vague desires and shape the best version of ourselves. Remember, the hero's journey can be demanding, but the rewards make the effort worthwhile.

The Gap Between Dreams and Reality

We all have dreams—vivid images of who we want to be, what we want to accomplish, and the life we envision. But the road from these visions to reality can be filled with obstacles. This disconnect is where our hopes often fade away. Why don't dreams always become reality? There are many reasons, so let's explore a few.

These Dreams

Dreams often originate from a place of idealism. They can appear as omens or visions. Often, dreams struggle to become reality because of our perceptions and lack of belief in ourselves. We don't realize our dreams because of self-doubt. Self-doubt can stem from various sources, including other people. It might come from yourself, especially if you were born into poverty, leaving you with a feeling of never catching up. It can also come from a partner, friend, or relative who doesn't want to see you succeed, and who is constantly telling you what you lack. Another reason dreams might not become reality is a lack of discipline or work ethic. For instance, someone might dream of becoming a world-famous musician but fail to consider the years of relentless practice, the crushing rejections, and the unpredictable nature of fame. An idealized view of a dream can lead to a harsh awakening when faced with the tougher realities of chasing our goals. We must constantly remind ourselves that anything worth having requires effort.

There is Nothing to Fear but Fear Itself

Fear is a powerful dream blocker. Fear of failure, fear of the unknown, fear of self-doubt—these can paralyze us, keeping us stuck in our comfort or discomfort.[1] Taking the first step toward a dream can feel like jumping into a void, and the fear of falling can prevent us from ever taking flight. But achieving anything often involves discomfort. For example, earning a college degree requires intensive study, sometimes when you'd rather be doing something else. Making a business successful demands countless hours of work and often rejection from various parties. And staying healthy involves eating right and exercising, even when you might want to simply 'pig out.'

Life of Limited Resources

Not all dreams are equal, and life isn't fair. We come from different backgrounds, and sometimes we take different paths to reach the same goal. Achieving our dreams may require financial, educational, or time resources, which might not be available to everyone. For instance, a lack of funds for medical school can block the dream of becoming a doctor. However, I believe that if being a doctor is your calling, limited resources shouldn't stop you from pursuing that dream.

Life's Priorities

Most of us know that life has a way of throwing curveballs. As we navigate adulthood, our priorities and perspectives often change. The dreams we cherished as children might not resonate with the adult we become. Family obligations, career demands, and the exhaustion of daily life can all push our dreams further down the to-do list until they fade into the background. I tell my children to prioritize their responsibilities because when they get married, their

---

1. Stepzinski, "Message of City's TEDx Conference."

priorities will shift or might even be moved to a back burner. When I was going through my divorce, I was invited to a program that would place me in front of top business schools offering a Ph.D. in business. But most of the schools wanted a total commitment to the program, so you had to be a full-time student, instead of also working a full-time job. As appealing as this opportunity was to me, I immediately declined because I would have had to leave my children. As I recall saying at the time, "I was not going to be a father who just sent a check." I was determined to be deeply involved in my children's upbringing, and looking back today on my decision, I have no regrets.

Your Dreams Are Never Dead

I believe there is timing in everything we do in life, and the difference between being able to go after our dreams or being unable to do so comes down to our present state of mind and abilities. For example, many athletes leave school early because they dream of making the NBA or NFL, but are they ready for the next level? Some make it, but most do not. Often, the difference maker for those who do not make it is that they didn't stay in school to improve their skills, which could better prepare them for the next level.

Depending on your dreams, rejection could be more impactful than it is for others. An athlete can't go back to college if they hire an agent and get cut from a team. My advice is to surround yourself with people who can offer wise counsel. I would also suggest imagining all possible outcomes, instead of only the one you hope for. And finally, and most importantly, I would pray for guidance and understanding. The gap between dreams and reality doesn't have to be insurmountable. Sometimes, as we mature, we might change course and adjust our dreams, which could lead to the best outcome for us. There's nothing wrong with changing your mind or taking a different path. Below are ways to better prepare you for pursuing your dream and remaining open-minded while accepting change in life.

- Refine the Dream: Not all dreams have to be grandiose. Maybe the dream of being a musician can be about learning a new instrument for personal enjoyment. Dreams can grow and change as our lives do.

- Embrace the Grind: Dreams take effort. There are no shortcuts to victory. Be ready to work hard, shed tears, and endure setbacks. Just remind yourself that the journey can be just as fulfilling as the destination.

- Embrace the Detours: Life rarely follows a straight path. Unexpected twists can lead to new and exciting opportunities. Perhaps the dream of playing in the NFL evolved into a coaching career, maybe even at another level.

- Celebrate the Small Wins: Don't be discouraged if you don't experience an immediate big victory. Every step forward and every hurdle you overcome is a win.

Ultimately, dreams serve a vital purpose, even if they are not realized in their exact form. They act as a spark, igniting our passions and pushing us forward. They give us something to strive for, a sense of purpose, and a guiding star through life. Even if we don't reach the exact destination we envisioned, the pursuit of our dreams shapes who we become, the skills we develop, and the resilience we build. So, the next time you find yourself musing about your dreams with a hint of longing, remember that the gap between them and reality doesn't have to be insurmountable. With a bit of drive, courage, and persistent self-improvement, you might surprise yourself with how much closer you can get to your aspirations.

Chapter 6: Own Your Future

Taking Responsibility

One of the best parts of college is that you can experience what it offers and discover more about yourself at the same time. Attending Eastern Kentucky University (EKU) in the fall of 1987 was a pivotal moment for me because I was away from home, and although my parents still supported me, I felt I had an extra level of independence—at least, I thought so. My parents were not there to wake me up to make sure I went to class, and I was free to make many of my own decisions, for better or worse!

When I attended EKU, it was considered a party school with a nationally ranked football team. I chose it because it offered a different atmosphere from the one my sisters and other relatives had experienced at Western Kentucky University

(WKU), which I visited many times in high school during spring breaks and homecomings. One of the most memorable times I spent there was hanging out with my cousin, Larry, and being around his fraternity brothers, the men of Alpha Phi Alpha Fraternity, Inc. They would brag about having the highest GPA and being scholars who made money. They also highlighted famous members, like Dr. Martin Luther King Jr., Supreme Court Justice Thurgood Marshall, and Olympic Champion Jesse Owens. Alpha Phi Alpha's rich history and the way its members carried themselves fueled my desire to join.

When I started at EKU, I prioritized settling into college life and figuring out when to study and when not to. I also aimed to learn more about Alpha Phi Alpha. Although there was no college chapter there, fraternity members were enrolled. Back then, fraternity members attending EKU had pledged at the University of Kentucky, so when I pledged, I had to go through the University of Kentucky, and I became a member on April 10, 1988.

After pledging, life felt new to me as an Alpha man. First and foremost, being an Alpha meant upholding high academic standards. I remember meeting some senior brothers at an event who were attorneys, and it felt like I was being pledged all over again. They welcomed me into the fraternity, but they were especially interested in my grades, plans, and life goals. Joining the fraternity also made me more well-known on campus. Although I've always been reserved, more people recognized me because I was an Alpha. That immediately made me more popular and more attractive to some women. Being young and receiving this extra attention boosted my confidence and stroked my ego. Unfortunately, my drinking also increased. Drinking before going to parties became routine, and I started to feel it was becoming excessive. I drank so much that sometimes I avoided looking in the mirror out of shame. I felt myself drifting away from the real Alan, and I knew I needed to improve and make a change. After all, college was a springboard for my future, and I had to be more responsible. I knew that if I didn't meet my parents' expectations, I'd be coming home in disgrace.

Time to Take Personal Responsibility for My Actions

Understanding personal responsibility is crucial for teenage and young adult males. It helps develop self-reliance and independence. Taking responsibility for your actions teaches you to depend on yourself to solve problems, make decisions, and reach your goals. This self-reliance is vital for building confidence and self-esteem, which are essential for success in all areas of life. In some cases, what I considered excessive drinking was really only one drink too many, but that was based on how I had been raised. Drinking was not permitted in my parents' house and is still not. I understood that drinking could lead to problems and get me in trouble. I knew the consequences and, more importantly, knew that was not the path I wanted to take. So, I realized I had to change my life. I needed to realign with who Alan was and what he stood for.

When Dad picked me up to go home for Christmas break in December 1988, I told him I hadn't been doing my best in school that semester and had decided to join the military reserves. He said okay, though I could tell he was thinking about the real reason why I told him I was not returning to school the following semester. Going into the reserves had always been on my mind because I served in the Junior ROTC in high school. I thought it would be a natural step because of the discipline and leadership skills I had developed over time. For example, I was promoted to company commander as a freshman, and we won the rifle competition, beating the upperclassmen.

When I arrived home, I contacted an Army recruiter and expressed my interest in learning more about the Army. He said he would come to my house in an hour, but he never showed up. The next day, I reached out to the Marines, and the recruiter was at my house within half an hour. I was sworn into the United States Marine Corps the day after that. I realized that joining the Marines would allow me to rediscover myself, regain my balance, and rebuild my life. My upbringing emphasized order and structure, and I was raised to value hard work and perseverance. Joining the Marines was a way for me to take personal responsibility, as I knew it would help reinforce a strong work ethic and a sense of purpose. I understood that I would undergo rigorous training that would instill purpose and direction in me, and it would also bring meaning to my life.

Graduating from boot camp was an accomplishment because it meant I had completed a difficult task, and equally important, I had taken personal responsibility by being determined to regain balance and focus. I also didn't have a desire to drink. I was back to being Alan, and I felt great! I was ready to serve and eager to return to EKU.

Being able to take personal responsibility is a great attribute because it forces you to see yourself from different perspectives. It took courage for me to admit that I had been wrong, that I could have done something differently, and that I needed to make a change. The sad reality is that teenagers and young adult males encounter many influences that cloud their judgment. For example, you might want to be part of the in-crowd to be popular, so you behave in ways that are not in your best interests, such as not focusing on school or pursuing a relationship with someone simply because they are beautiful. But does that in-crowd or that beautiful person share your values and interests? I know you're young and still figuring out who you are, but now is the time to look in the mirror and ask yourself who you are and what you want out of life.

Taking control of your life by accepting responsibility opens the door for you to see more clearly where you want to go and what you aim for. It does not mean you won't make mistakes or experience failure. What it means is that you will be better prepared to handle challenges because you'll be stable. And when you become a better version of yourself, you will develop a stronger sense of awareness and wisdom, which will help you avoid saying and doing things that do not serve you well.

Cultivating Positive Habits and Behaviors

Life is about making choices, and every choice has consequences. For example, if you work out four times a week, you will eventually get in better shape. On the flip side, if you drink alcohol heavily, you will more than likely develop health issues. As teenagers, there are many decisions you must make, and they can be either good or bad for you. During the teenage years, the brain undergoes significant changes, and the prefrontal cortex, responsible for decision-making, impulse control, and reasoning, is still developing. This means you may not always make sound decisions and might engage in risky behavior. Hormonal changes during puberty also contribute to mood swings and emotional instability. Physically, you are still growing and maturing. You may experience growth spurts and changes in your body shape and size. These physical changes can affect your self-esteem and body image. During this time, it is extremely important that parents, guardians, and other adults guide and support you as you navigate this stage of life.

Building a Strong Foundation: Positive Habits and Behaviors for Teenage Boys

As a teenager, I struggled with my confidence and self-esteem. I was shy and thought there was something wrong with that. It didn't reach the point of having anxiety, but it was something I noticed. I accepted the changes in myself—physically, mentally, and emotionally—mainly because I always focused on doing or being involved with activities like football and track. As I mentioned before, I dedicated a lot of time to being the best I could be, so the more I worked, the better my results. Seeing positive results made me feel good, and the more I did it, the more it became a habit. The behaviors I followed started to reduce my self-esteem issues. Looking back, my self-esteem issues were really about transitioning from a boy into a man and learning to accept who I am. It was a transformation of my mindset—one where I had to speak words of affirmation and support myself with positive things.

Defining the Positive

Positive behaviors are actions that contribute to your overall personal growth and development. They promote physical and mental health, build strong relationships, and foster a sense of responsibility and accomplishment. Being positive is a mental state that can influence our actions. For example, I worked with someone I did not get along with. Because of my negative view of this person, I would often think about how I would confront them. My mind became so focused on my dislike for them that I had to step back, pray, and ask God to remove all negative thoughts from my mind. Thankfully, He answered my prayer, and I was able to think more clearly about how to work with that person despite lingering anger. The lesson I learned from this was that when we are upset or have negative thoughts, it hinders us from operating at our best, which is why it is best to think and stay positive as much as possible. Of course, being positive is a mindset and practice that must be continually nurtured. Here are some key aspects of positive behavior:

- Health and Wellness: Prioritizing a healthy lifestyle goes a long way. This includes getting enough sleep (around 8-10 hours), eating nutritious meals, and engaging in regular physical activity. Taking care of your body fuels your mind and sets the stage for a healthy future.

- Academics: Dedicating time to studies and developing good learning habits are essential. This involves setting goals, managing time effectively, and actively participating in class. Strong academic performance opens doors to future opportunities.

- Responsibility: Taking ownership of your actions and commitments demonstrates maturity. This includes completing chores at home, being on time for school and appointments, and respecting deadlines. Being responsible builds trust and fosters a sense of accomplishment.

- Respect: Treating others with respect, regardless of age or background, is fundamental. This includes actively listening, using kind words, and valuing other people's opinions. Respectful behavior creates a positive environment for everyone.

- Communication: Being able to communicate your thoughts and feelings effectively is vital. This involves expressing yourself clearly, listening attentively, and having open and honest conversations. Strong communication skills strengthen relationships and are critical to managing life's challenges.

- Positivity: Cultivating a positive outlook allows you to handle problems with resilience. Having a positive attitude helps you see the bright side, find solutions, and build confidence in yourself.

Identifying the Negative

Have you ever noticed that negative things typically attract a lot of attention? Reality shows, for example, are full of drama and conflicts, but they always have high ratings. Negative behaviors hinder growth and development, but people are nevertheless drawn to them. The reality is, negativity can negatively affect your health, relationships, and future opportunities. Recognizing when you are in a negative mindset is the first step toward positive change, and this will lead to taking action to turn negatives into positives. Some common negative behaviors among teenage boys include:

- Unhealthy Habits: Indulging in excessive screen time, poor sleep patterns, unhealthy eating habits, and lack of physical activity can have detrimental effects on health and well-being.

- Academic Neglect: Skipping classes, failing to complete assignments, and lacking motivation in studies can hinder academic success and limit future opportunities.

- Irresponsibility: Neglecting chores, procrastinating on tasks, and being unreliable can damage relationships with family and friends. It also hinders your ability to manage time effectively and build trust.

- Disrespect: Disrespectful behavior includes bullying, name-calling, making offensive jokes, or being inconsiderate of others. It creates a negative atmosphere and damages relationships.

- Poor Communication: Difficulty expressing yourself clearly, interrupting others, or being dismissive of their opinions can lead to misunderstandings and conflict.

- Mismanagement of Money: Failing to manage money can lead to significant stress and limited life options.

- Negativity: Maintaining a consistently negative outlook can drain your energy and limit your ability to recognize opportunities. It can also discourage others around you.

Building Positive Habits by Acting

Cultivating positive habits takes time and effort, but the rewards are worth it.[1] There have been myths about how long it takes, such as the commonly quoted "21 days" myth.[2] This originated with plastic surgeon Maxwell Maltz, who observed that patients took about 21 days to adjust to changes. Changing your habit(s) really depends upon your behavior and focus.[3] I would not recommend trying to accomplish goals on day one; instead, take a systematic approach to achieve your goals. Below is a step-by-step guide to help you get started:

---

1. Mosunic, "Learn How Long It Takes."

2. Selk, "Habit Formation: The 21-Day Myth."

3. Clear, "How Long Does It Actually Take."

1. Identify Your Goals: What areas of your life do you want to improve? Do you want to boost your grades, get in better shape, or improve your communication skills? Setting clear goals will help you focus your efforts.

2. Research Best Practices: Identifying your goals is a good start, but knowing how to reach them is even better. Search the web for how best to reach your goals. You'll find many different practices and suggestions, so choose the strategies that you think will work best for you.

3. Start Small: Don't try to overhaul your life overnight. Begin with small, manageable changes or micro steps that you can realistically stick with. For example, to become more fit, try adding a 30-minute walk to your daily routine, or to improve academically, dedicate an hour every day to studying after school.

4. Find Support: Having a support system will make this process easier. Talk to your parents, teachers, significant other or a trusted friend about your goals and ask for their encouragement.

5. Track Your Progress: Keeping track of your progress will help you stay motivated. This can be done using a journal, a habit tracker app, or simply sharing your progress with your support system.

6. Celebrate Your Successes: Acknowledge and celebrate even small wins. This reinforces positive behavior and keeps you motivated to continue.

7. Be Patient with Yourself: Change takes time. There will almost certainly be setbacks along the way. Don't get discouraged – learn from your mistakes and keep pushing forward.

Taking responsibility for your future is a sure-fire way to achieve success in life. It reminds me of the famous proverb my parents often repeat: "The early bird gets the worm," meaning those who wake up early and prepare ahead will have an advantage. To take responsibility, you need to plan for your future and get ready for it. Don't forget to build relationships. For example, if you're in high school and want to become a pilot, an astronaut, a scientist, or even a writer, attending summer camps or specialized schools can give you valuable exposure to whatever field you're interested in. This exposure can provide insight into what it's like to be in that profession. You might also consider taking courses that prepare you for your chosen career. For instance, if you want to be a doctor, you'll need to study the sciences; if you hope to be an engineer, being proficient in math is mandatory. Growing your network and joining clubs related to your interests can also be extremely helpful. If your school doesn't have a club that meets your needs, take the initiative to start one. For example, the CollegeVine website features an article about 70 clubs you can start now.[4] Whatever path you choose, have a plan for how to reach your goals. If you're unsure how to proceed, ask a teacher or counselor for guidance. You can do it—so let's get started today!

---

4. Weintraub, "70 High School Clubs."

Chapter 7: Hustle Smart
Mastering Your Finances

When I was nine, a huge snowstorm blanketed the city. Over twelve inches of snow were on the ground, the streets were covered with ice, and schools were canceled. Many days passed, and I was so bored that cabin fever was around the corner, and I didn't know what to do. Then I had a bright idea: "I am going to make some money by shoveling snow! So, I hit the streets, bundled in layers against the biting wind, and became a one-man snow shoveling force. I went door to door, asking my neighbors if I could shovel their snow for a fee. Hours melted away as I wrestled with drifts, shovel scraping relentlessly against the snow-covered, icy pavement, while staying out for hours at a time. My hands grew numb, and my feet were like ice blocks, but I wouldn't stop. Each house cleared brought a surge of accomplishment, a tiny victory against the winter's wrath. When I completed a job, I felt proud that I had accomplished a task. When the day ended, I would rush home and excitedly tell my parents what I had done. They would listen attentively and encourage me to continue what I was doing. They put my shoveling money in a savings account. A small seed was planted that first day, the birth of my relentless spirit, the beginning of the "hustle" that would forever define me.

Summer arrived, replacing the snow with a suffocating blanket of heat. The boredom of winter may have been relentless, but this was a different beast entirely. Sweat dripped off my head as I pushed the lawnmower. I was at it again, hustling to make money. For starters, I wanted leather basketball shoes, or as we called them, tennis shoes, and I wanted a pair because all the star basketball players wore them, even though, to this day, my brother says my style of playing basketball was football on a basketball court. Nonetheless, I wanted to be cool (or what I believed was cool). So, I worked and bought myself a pair. That was one of the few things I wanted, and I was content with it. Even today, I am not driven by a desire for clothing, though I do enjoy being fashionable, just at a reasonable price!

I would shovel snow and mow lawns for several years, though I cut down on doing it during my high school years because I was involved in sports throughout the year. During the summer of my junior year, my then brother-in-law got me a job in the dish room at Blue Bore Cafeteria. I worked there for about a month. I only made minimum wage, which was around $3.35 an hour at that time. It was a dirty job, and I did not like it, mainly because I would leave smelling like every piece of food I had eaten there.

My senior year rolled around, and I started dating the lady who later became my wife, Doris. I wanted to take her out to eat and to the movies, and even though I wasn't into the clubs, I would occasionally go to them. I would ask my parents for money to go out, but that only happened a couple of times because Dad came to me and clearly said he wasn't going to give me money to take my date out and burn up the car's gas. So, I knew I had to get a job.

I told my classmate Lewis about my need for a job, and he said that our other classmate, Bobby, had a job working at the Courier-Journal Newspaper, selling door-to-door subscriptions to the paper. Bobby talked about how cool and fun the job was, and Lewis and I were sold, so we both applied for the sales position and were hired.

The job paid an hourly wage plus commission, and Bobby had not lied; it was fun. Part of what made it fun was that we had a great supervisor, Gregg. He knew we were young and energetic, and he was always sharing pearls of wisdom with us, and we listened. There were minimum sales standards, but for the most part, we consistently achieved our goals because the commissions were handsome.

I worked at the Courier-Journal from January of my senior year until I went to college, and during that time, I made a nice amount of money. Unfortunately, I did not manage it properly because I was preoccupied with buying clothes and dating. What got my attention was when Dad asked how much I made, how much I saved, and what my priorities were. I told him, and he told me that I was going in the wrong direction in managing my money. That was the beginning of my learning and understanding that I needed to change how I manage my finances.

You Are Never Too Young to Start Being the Boss of Your Money

Mowing lawns to make money became a routine for me during my teenage years. During that time, I earned about $30 to $50 a week, which was pretty good money for the time. I also acquired various skills: I acquired the essential abilities to market myself, negotiate prices effectively, and sharpen my customer service skills, using every customer issue as a chance to learn. Though I was new to these skills, I sharpened them and still use them today. My cousin Larry even picked up the same skills during his junior and senior years in high school. As he became busier with college, he asked me to take over his yard business, and I jumped at the opportunity! I was punctual and reliable. From that experience, I learned that when you offer a product or service, you will please some customers, but you cannot always please everyone. Of all the yards I mowed, one customer didn't like how I did her yard. She complained that I didn't cut it like Larry did. I was young and became defensive, but in reality, it was a learning moment for me. I realized that the key was understanding her expectations, such as the height or pattern Larry used when mowing her lawn.

It's Not About How Much You Make but What You Do with It

While I earned money by cutting lawns, what mattered most was what I did with it. That was important because Dad used to say, "It is not about how much money you make, but what you do with what you make." While we all know that how much money you make is very important, his point was about how we manage our money. Do you value money and have the discipline to handle it? Much like anything worth having, managing your money wisely requires discipline. Sadly, with all the ads, social media, and celebrities promoting the image of living a great life, with beautiful homes, expensive cars, and designer clothes, many people crave that kind of lifestyle and want those material things right away. I recall discussing with students the importance of understanding what they read and managing their finances effectively. I asked one student, "If you were in the entertainment (rap) business, and you signed a contract with me and I gave you $50,000.00, how would you handle it?" He excitedly began listing all the things he would buy. Then I asked how he would feel if I told him I had made $2 million from his music. He got upset and said we would need to have another conversation about his money. That's when I explained to him and the rest of the class why it's crucial to understand what you're reading and to know your worth.

Budgeting Is Key

You can earn $25,000 a year or $10 million a year, but if you don't have a budget and know how to manage it, you'll end up broke. Very little in today's culture can be counted on to remain secure. Jobs, for example, don't have the same lifespan they once had, and sadly, marriages might not last 'until death do you part' anymore, as divorce rates continue to rise. Today, more than ever, we must take control of our own finances, and budgeting is the first step.

No doubt you've heard the word thrown around, but you might still be wondering what exactly budgeting means, especially to you. Budgeting is basically like creating a spending plan for your money. For example, when you plan a road trip, you don't just hop in the car without knowing where you're going or how much gas you'll need, right? Budgeting will help you figure out how much money you have coming in (like from your job or allowance), and allow you to decide how you'll spend it, for example, on essentials (like food and rent) and non-essentials (like video games, new shoes or a new phone). Below are the steps for creating a budget.

Step 1: Track Your Spending

- Gather your financial records, including bank statements, credit card bills, receipts, and any other documentation of your spending.

- Categorize your expenses: Divide your spending into categories like housing, transportation, food, utilities, entertainment, and savings.

- Use budgeting tools: Consider using budgeting apps (like Mint or Personal Capital), spreadsheets (like Google Sheets or Excel), or even a simple notebook to track your spending.

Step 2: Determine Your Net Monthly Income

- Calculate your take-home pay: Subtract taxes and any other deductions from your gross (pre-tax) monthly income.

- Factor in other income sources: Include any extra income you receive, from things like side hustles, investments, or rental income.

Step 3: List Your Monthly Expenses

- Fixed Expenses: These are expenses that stay the same each month, such as:

  - Rent or mortgage

  - Utilities (electricity, water, gas, internet)

  - Insurance (health, car, renters)

  - Loan payments (student loans, car loans)

- Variable Expenses: These are expenses that can change each month, such as:

  - Groceries

  - Transportation (gas, public transportation)

  - Dining out/Ordering in

  - Entertainment

  - Shopping

Step 4: Create a Budget Plan

- Allocate funds to each expense category: Based on your priorities and spending habits, assign a specific amount of money to each category.

- The 50/30/20 Rule: A common budgeting guideline is to allocate 50% of your income to needs (housing, utilities, groceries), 30% to wants (dining out, entertainment, hobbies), and 20% to savings and debt repayment.[1]

- Consider budgeting methods:

  - 50/30/20 Rule: See above.

  - Zero-Based Budgeting: Allocate every dollar of your income to a specific expense or savings goal, ensuring you spend only what you earn.[2]

  - Envelope System: Physically divide your cash into envelopes for different expense categories.

Step 5: Track Your Progress and Make Necessary Adjustments

- Regularly review your budget: Compare your actual spending to your budgeted amounts.

- Identify areas where you can cut back: Look for areas where you can reduce spending without significantly impacting your quality of life.

---

1. Warren and Tyagi, *All Your Worth*.

2. Ramsey, *Financial Peace Revisited*.

- Adjust your budget as needed: Life changes, so your budget should evolve with you. Adjust your budget plan as your income or expenses change.

Example using $4,000 as a Monthly Income:

- Estimate of Expenses:

    ◦ Rent/Mortgage: $1,500

    ◦ Utilities: $200

    ◦ Groceries: $300

    ◦ Transportation: $300

    ◦ Dining Out/Entertainment: $600

    ◦ Savings: $500

    ◦ Debt Repayment: $300

- Total Estimated Expenses: $3,700

- Available Funds: $4,000 - $3, 700 = $300

This leaves you with $300 of discretionary income each month. You can use this for unexpected expenses, to increase savings, or to treat yourself.

Important Notes:

- Be realistic: Don't create a budget that is too restrictive or unrealistic to maintain.

- Be patient: Finding the best budgeting system for you may take some time.

- Stay motivated: Remember to celebrate your successes, and don't get discouraged by setbacks.

This framework can help you create a budget that aligns with your financial goals and maximizes your monthly income, regardless of its amount.

Owning Your Finances

As I grew up, I made some smart financial moves as well as some less-than-smart moves. This is why I can now advise you to own your finances and to tell you that you are never too young to start planning and acting. Owning your finances is about being disciplined and having the know-how to position your money so that it accumulates through an interest-bearing instrument. In other words, it's a good idea to put some savings in an investment component so it will grow over time. There are several investment instruments that compound interest over time. Below are the various types.

Low-Risk Saving Instruments

Savings Accounts

A savings account is simply a bank account where you can save your money. It's like a piggy bank but with a little interest. Anyone of any age can open a savings account, but generally cannot open one on their own until they are 18, the legal age in most states. You can start with as little as a few dollars. Interest rates are usually pretty low, so it takes a while to see any real growth, but the risk is very low. Your money is safe in a bank.

Money Market Accounts

A money market account offers slightly higher interest rates than a savings account. You can usually write checks from it. Typically, you need to be an adult to open a money market account and usually need a higher starting balance than a regular savings account. Interest rates are better than those of a regular savings account, but are still relatively low, and so is the risk. The FDIC (Federal Deposit Insurance Corporation, the government agency that insures bank deposits) still insures your money.[3]

Certificates of Deposit (CDs)

CDs are a type of savings account in which you agree to leave your money in the bank for a specific period of time (like six months or a year) in exchange for a higher interest rate. Anyone can open a CD. The minimum amount to open a CD can vary, but it's usually more than a savings account. Interest rates are generally higher than those in savings accounts, but you cannot access your money during the specified time period. This is also a low-risk investment, and your money is insured by the FDIC.

Savings Bonds

Savings bonds are a debt security issued by the government. In other words, you lend the government money for a specific period, and they pay you interest. Anyone can buy savings bonds in any denomination. Interest rates are generally low but steady, and the risk is very low as well, as they are backed by the U.S. government.

Traditional Investments

Stocks

Stocks are like owning a tiny piece of a company. If the company does well, your stock can increase in value, and you might also be paid dividends. You generally have to be at least 18 years old to buy stock, but you can start with as little as one share, although building a diversified portfolio might take some time with this

---

3. FDIC, "Deposit Insurance at a Glance."

amount. There is potential for high returns, but it can take years, as stock prices go up and down. The stock market can be volatile, and you can lose money, so the risk is generally high.[4]

Traditional (Fix-Income) Bonds

A bond is basically a loan to a company or government. You get paid interest regularly, and when the bond matures, you get your original investment back. You can invest in bonds at any age. Bond prices vary, and returns are usually lower than stocks, but they're also less risky, though not risk-free. Bond prices can go down.

Mutual Funds

A mutual fund is like a basket of stocks, bonds, or other investments. Professional financial planners manage it. You can start investing in mutual funds as soon as you have some money. Many mutual funds have low minimum investments, making them accessible to most people. Returns can vary depending on what's in the fund. Generally, they're less risky than individual stocks, but the risk varies depending on the fund.

Exchange-traded funds (ETFs)

Like mutual funds, these funds trade on the stock exchange like a stock. You can invest in ETFs as soon as you can buy and sell stocks, and like individual stocks, you can start with a small amount. Returns can vary, but ETFs often track a specific index, like the S&P 500. The risk varies depending on the ETF, but generally it is lower than individual stocks.

Real Estate

Owning property or investing in real estate through REITs (Real Estate Investment Trusts) is yet another type of investment to consider. There's no

---

4. Investopedia, "Stocks: What They Are."

specific age to start investing in real estate, but it can be expensive, so you might need a larger initial amount. There is potential for high returns through rent, appreciation, and tax benefits, but the risk is high because real estate can be illiquid, and property values can fluctuate.

Annuities

An annuity is a contract with an insurance company that provides you with a steady income stream, often in retirement. You can buy an annuity at any age, but they're often used for retirement planning.

The amount you need to invest depends on the type of annuity and the income you want. The return depends on the annuity type. Some offer guaranteed returns, while others are linked to market performance. The risk also varies depending on the annuity type. Fixed annuities are generally low-risk, while variable annuities carry more risk.

Real Estate Investment Trusts (REITs)

As mentioned above, REITs are a way to invest in real estate without buying a building yourself. They own properties like apartments, offices, or shopping centers and share the profits with investors. You can invest in REITs as soon as you can buy stocks, and start with a relatively small amount, since you can buy just one share. REITs often provide steady income through dividends, and their value can also increase over time. Generally, REITs are considered less risky than investing in individual properties, but they're still subject to market fluctuations.

Alternative Investments

Commodities

Commodities are raw materials like gold, oil, or agricultural products. You can invest in them through futures contracts or by buying shares in companies that produce them. You can invest in commodities at any age, but it's often considered a more complex investment. Commodity investments can vary in cost, from relatively low for futures contracts to higher for physical commodities. These carry the potential for high returns, but are also high risk, as commodity prices can fluctuate wildly based on supply and demand.

Cryptocurrencies

Digital or virtual currencies like Bitcoin, Ethereum, and others are collectively called cryptocurrencies. While there's no age restriction, most platforms require you to be an adult to invest. You can start with a small amount, but cryptocurrency prices can be volatile. There is potential for very high returns but also a high risk of loss because cryptocurrency is a highly speculative market.

Collectibles

Items like art, antiques, or rare coins that may appreciate in value over time are another vehicle for investing. There's no age restriction but building a valuable collection often takes time. The cost of collectibles varies widely. There is potential for high returns, but it can be difficult to sell collectibles.

The value of collectibles can fluctuate, making it challenging to find buyers, so the risk is high.

Crowdfunding

Crowdfunding is investing in startups or projects through online platforms. Age restrictions vary by platform, but typically, you need to be an adult. Investment amounts can be small, though, which makes this vehicle accessible to many. There is potential for high returns, but the majority of crowdfunded projects fail, so the risk is very high.

Peer-to-Peer Lending

Lending money to individuals or businesses through online platforms is called peer-to-peer lending.[5] Typically, you need to be an adult to invest in peer-to-peer lending, but you can start with relatively small amounts. There is potential for higher returns than traditional savings accounts, but also higher risk, as borrowers may default on their loans.

Retirement Accounts

401(k)

This is a retirement savings plan offered by your employer. You contribute a portion of your paycheck, and often, your employer matches a percentage of that portion. You can start contributing to a 401(k) as soon as your employer offers it. The amount you contribute depends on your income and savings goals. Many plans allow you to start with small amounts. Returns depend on the investment options you choose within the plan. Since this is a long-term investment, the aim is for growth over time. The risk varies based on the investment options you select, so diversification can help manage it.[6]

Individual Retirement Account (IRA)

An IRA is a personal retirement savings account that offers tax advantages. You can typically open an IRA at any age. Contribution limits exist, but you can often start with small amounts. Returns depend on the investments you choose, but IRAs are designed for long-term growth, and the risk varies based on your investments.

---

5. Huang, "Development of a Risk Model," 192–96.

6. IRS, "401(k) Plan Overview."

Roth IRA

This is a type of IRA in which you contribute after-tax dollars. Your contributions grow tax-free, and qualified withdrawals in retirement are tax-free. You can contribute to a Roth IRA up to a certain income level. Contribution limits exist, but you can often start with small amounts. Returns depend on the investments you choose, so the risk varies.

Making Your Money Work for You

I often hear people say they are getting their hustle or grind on, but for what? The reasons vary, from short-term goals like buying a new car, boat, or going on vacation, to saving for a house or college. Some people are hustling to survive or maintain a certain lifestyle. I applaud people who have the discipline to work and hustle for extra income, and if others are depending on your income, you should maximize your earnings by working two jobs. I say this because I'm sure you want to build yourself a nest egg and save for a rainy day.

As you work to save and invest your money, my advice is to have a plan for growing it. For example, imagine putting the money you save in a shoebox under your bed. If you leave it there, it might survive, but it won't grow. But when you save and invest your money, it will grow into something much greater. Saving and investing aren't just about accumulating wealth; they're about creating a life where money works for you rather than the other way around. They're about building a financial foundation that provides security, freedom, and opportunities.

Here's why you should let your money start working for you:

1. Beat Inflation: Inflation is like a silent thief. It gradually erodes the purchasing power of your money over time. By saving and investing, you can outpace inflation, preserving the value of your hard-earned dollars.

2. Achieve Your Goals: Whether buying a home, starting a business, or retiring comfortably, saving and investing both bring you closer to your dreams. You'll be amazed at what you can accomplish by setting financial goals and creating a plan.

3. Build an Emergency Fund: Life is unpredictable. Unexpected expenses like medical bills or car repairs can come up out of the blue. An emergency fund acts as a safety net, preventing you from going into debt during tough times.

4. Create a Secure Retirement: Social Security might not be enough to cover your retirement expenses. Saving and investing for your golden years ensures a comfortable lifestyle without financial worries.

5. Legacy Building: Want to leave a financial legacy for your children or loved ones? Saving and investing can help you achieve that goal. By building wealth, you can provide opportunities for future generations.

Remember, starting small is okay. Even saving a little bit each month can make a big difference over time. The key is consistency and discipline. By making saving and investing a habit, you're taking control of your financial future and setting yourself up for long-term success.

Having a Plan and Working Your Plan

While growing up, Dad would always say to me, "You have to have a plan, Alan." And he was right! You have to have a plan for everything you do. What is important is how you are going to live your life and handle your finances. I am a firm believer in planning, but I also have action steps and attainable goals. Attainable means realistic. For example, it might be realistic to say your goal is to make one million dollars in five years if you have the resources and systems in place to make it, but is it realistic to say you are going to make that million by just sitting at home thinking it will fall out of the sky and into your lap without a plan? Of course not!

Whatever you desire to achieve financially requires discipline and consistency. Below is a 6-month plan to help you stay focused and on track to achieve your budgetary and financial goals.

6-Month Plan for Budgeting & Financial Health

This plan focuses on building a sustainable budget, tracking spending effectively, and implementing strategies to save and reduce debt.

Month 1: Foundation & Assessment

- Track Spending:

  - Method: Use a budgeting app and record every single expense, no matter how small.

- Income Analysis:

  - Determine your monthly take-home pay after taxes and deductions.

- Expense Categorization:

  - Categorize your spending (housing, food, transportation, entertainment, etc.) to identify spending patterns.

Month 2: Budgeting Basics

- Create a Budget:

  - 50/30/20 Rule and adjust as needed: Review your spending from Month 1 and adjust your budget accordingly.

- Set Financial Goals:

  - Short-term (e.g., emergency fund, vacation) and long-term (e.g., retirement, down payment).

Month 3: Automation & Savings

- Automate Savings:

  - Set up automatic transfers to savings and investment accounts.

- Emergency Fund:

  - Aim for 3-6 months of living expenses in an easily accessible account.

- Debt Reduction Strategies:

  - Avalanche Method: Prioritize paying down the highest-interest debt first.

  - Snowball Method: Prioritize paying off the smallest debts first for motivation.

Month 4: Spending Review & Adjustments

- Review Spending:

  - Analyze your spending from the past month.

  - Identify areas where you can cut back (e.g., dining out, subscriptions).

- Budget Refinement:

  - Make necessary adjustments to your budget based on your spending review.

Month 5: Debt Reduction Focus

- Intensify Debt Repayment:

  - Explore options like debt consolidation or balance transfers.

  - Consider a side hustle to generate extra income for debt repayment.

- Negotiate Lower Interest Rates:

  - Contact creditors to negotiate lower interest rates on your loans.

Month 6: Maintenance & Refinement

- Regularly Review & Adjust:

  - Review your budget and spending habits on a weekly or monthly basis.

  - Make adjustments as needed based on changes in income or expenses.

- Celebrate Successes:

  - Acknowledge and reward your progress towards your financial goals.

Disclaimer: This is a general plan. Adjust it to fit your specific financial situation and goals. This information is for general guidance only and does not constitute financial advice. For personalized recommendations, consult with a qualified financial advisor.

Chapter 8: Forge Your Own Path

Building Your Career

The beauty of being a teenager is that you can explore different career options to find out what you like and don't like. For instance, I remember becoming fascinated with airplanes in the 6th grade, and my science teacher, Ms. O'Keefe, whose husband was a pilot, would bring me his pilot magazines to read. I thought it would be exciting to become a fighter pilot, but after flying in a plane during stormy weather, I quickly changed my mind! Like many boys who played sports, I wanted to go to college and play professional football. Playing sports kept my interest throughout high school and helped me maintain good grades because I knew my father would remove me from the team if my grades slipped. I also joined Navy ROTC in high school and was promoted to platoon commander during my freshman year. I enjoyed it, and it was a natural fit for me because the rules aligned with how I had been brought up. Being in ROTC also led me to the decision to join the military while in college.

In college, I chose to major in law enforcement because of the challenge and excitement I believed there would be in this type of career. The TV shows I watched, for instance, led me to pursue that career path; I envisioned myself as a police officer at either the local or federal level. But so often in life, the road you travel will reveal to you the direction you should go, and for me, this was my deployment in the Persian Gulf War. While there, I spent a considerable amount of time reading and discussing our culture and societal expectations with fellow Marines. We talked about both the good and bad aspects of society, and from that point on, I wanted to make a difference by helping others. Of course, there are many ways to do this, but I knew I needed to align my strengths and talents to be as effective as possible.

Discovering Your Gifts and Purpose

Have you ever wondered what your unique purpose is in this world? Have you felt a pull toward something, a passion that ignites your soul? Chances are, you have gifts, talents, and abilities waiting to be discovered. If you're a teenager who plays sports, you might dream of becoming a sports star, but how do you know if that is your true purpose? Asking someone about their purpose can be challenging because people often don't explore or reflect on it; instead, it is revealed naturally through their actions. For example, Lamar Jackson is an exceptionally talented quarterback in the NFL because of his athletic abilities. When he runs the ball, he is so quick that he often leaves defenders gasping for air as they try to tackle him or losing their balance and falling as they try to keep up with his moves. There's no need to question whether excelling in football is part of his purpose because it's obvious he is excellent at the sport.

But how do you know your purpose, especially when you don't see it clearly or you're determined to make it to the NFL, but might not be able to match that level of skill? Many boys love playing sports, and they know the money sports professionals make, and they're attracted to the glitz and glamour that come with it. Some parents even push their children to play sports, seeing it as a way to make a fortune or pull them out of poverty. I would never discourage a kid from pursuing their dreams, but I always advise keeping your options open. We all possess various talents that are part of our purpose, but nothing lasts forever, so you need to have options.

The tricky part of understanding our purpose is that we often think it should be a world-changing journey, or that we should be famous, or that we should impact millions of lives, or that we should make millions of dollars. If that doesn't happen or we have to work overtime for it, we might start to think it's not our true purpose. The truth is, your mission may serve a different purpose from the one you first imagined, and may simply be aligned with different circumstances, people, or communities than you expected.

We are all born with a unique combination of strengths and passions. These are your gifts, your superpowers. They're the things that come naturally to you, that you enjoy doing, and that you're good at. I think of my son, Hilton, for instance. He recently graduated from college with a degree in computer science and engineering. This field was easy for him because he enjoys working on computers. In high school, he built his own computer and created animated computer games as a hobby. He also really enjoys playing the piano and painting. I want the best for him, and while I pray that he has a successful career in his chosen field, I can certainly envision him playing in a band as a weekend hobby while working as an engineer.

What are your gifts? Close your eyes and think about the activities that bring you joy and fulfillment. What are you naturally drawn to? What tasks do you effortlessly excel at? Perhaps you're a natural-born leader, inspiring and motivating others with ease. Perhaps you have a knack for problem-solving and finding creative solutions to complex challenges. Or maybe you have a gift for connecting with people and building strong relationships wherever you go.

If you're struggling to pinpoint your gifts, don't worry. Very few people know with certainty early in life what they are meant to do. Here are some ways to uncover your hidden talents:

- Reflect on your past: Consider the activities you loved as a child. What were you passionate about? Did you enjoy painting, writing, or building things? These early interests might hold clues to your gifts.

- Identify your strengths: What are you naturally good at? Are you organized, analytical, or creative? These strengths can be a starting point for discovering your gifts.

- Pay attention to your passions: What excites you? What makes you lose track of time? Your passions often align with your gifts.

- Seek feedback: Ask friends, family, or colleagues what they think your strengths are. Sometimes, others can see our talents more clearly than we can.

- Try new things: Explore different activities outside your comfort zone. You might discover hidden talents you never knew existed.

Once you've identified your gifts, the next step is to nurture and develop them. Begin by setting small goals to enhance your skills. Practice consistently, seek feedback, and learn from others.

Remember, your gifts are meant to be shared with the world. Find ways to use your talents to make a positive impact, whether through your career, volunteer work, or hobbies. Let your gifts shine.

Discovering and developing your gifts is a journey, not a destination. It's about self-discovery, growth, and fulfillment. Embrace the process, and you'll be amazed at what you can achieve.

Seeking Wise Counsel to Put Your Gifts and Purpose to Work

I firmly believe we should seek wise counsel throughout our life to learn and confirm our direction. The key is understanding how to absorb the information given and use it to your advantage. You also need to know how to distinguish useful from non-useful information. I have learned a lot from people from all walks of life: my father, my track coach, the men at my job, and the men at my church. Seeking wise counsel helps prevent costly mistakes. For example, while I was completing my Master of Public Administration (MPA) degree, a Vice President at the University of Louisville at the time told me that it's great to have an MPA, but having one without connections is like having only a quarter in your pocket. He said I needed to network and sell the skills I could offer. We also need people who are our cheerleaders—those with influence who can speak on our behalf. It's wonderful to have people vouch for you, but you must make deposits with them to thank them for advocating for you. Volunteering, job shadowing, and informational interviews are excellent ways to connect and build relationships. These experiences provide opportunities to listen and learn about how that person advanced into their role and what obstacles to avoid. I've found that conducting informational interviews can be incredibly helpful in developing relationships because most people enjoy sharing how they rose to their current position.

Informational Interviews

An informational interview involves calling the person of your choice, introducing yourself, and thanking them for taking the time to speak with you. If you cannot connect by phone, try emailing them. Tell them you're seeking a career in their field and would like to learn more about how they advanced to their current role. Since you're basically asking for a favor and their time, it's important to be flexible with their schedule. The interview can either be in person or over the phone. Once you've agreed on a date and time, make sure you're prepared and ask questions about their background and how they achieved their success. Below are some sample questions.

Career Path and Role

1. Can you tell me about your career path so far? What steps did you take to progress from your early roles to your current position?

2. What were the key turning points or decisions that shaped your path? How did these choices impact your professional growth?

3. Could you describe a typical day in your current role? What are the primary responsibilities and challenges?

Industry and Company Insights

1. What are the most significant trends and challenges facing the industry today?

2. How has the industry evolved over the past few years? What do you anticipate for the future?

3. What do you enjoy most about working at your company? What sets it apart from competitors?

Skills and Qualifications

1. What skills or qualifications do you believe are essential for success in this field?

2. What advice would you give to someone interested in pursuing a career in this industry?

3. Are there any specific certifications or advanced degrees that you rec-

ommend?

Networking and Career Advancement

1. How important is networking in this industry?

2. Can you share some networking strategies that have been effective for you?

An informational interview helps break the ice and could potentially lead to a business relationship with your interviewee. After your interview, it's a good idea to send them a *handwritten* thank-you note. This can be the start of developing a connection that might open up future opportunities. The important part is to stay in touch with your interviewee, even in small ways. For example, if you have their cell number and know their birthday, just text a simple "Happy Birthday," or "Happy Thanksgiving," "Merry Christmas," and so on. These are thoughtful ways to keep the connection and to stay on their mind.

Building and maintaining relationships forged through informational interviews is crucial for career growth. Below are steps to help nurture these connections:

Immediate Follow-Up

- Send a timely thank-you note: Express your gratitude for their time and insights.

- Summarize key points: Briefly recap the most valuable information you gained from the conversation.

- Reiterate your interest: Confirm your enthusiasm for the field and the company.

Stay Connected

- Join relevant professional networks: Connect on platforms like LinkedIn.

- Share articles or industry news: Demonstrate your continued interest in the field.

- Offer assistance: If appropriate, offer to help with a small task or project.

Build Mutual Benefits

- Seek advice when needed: Don't hesitate to reach out if you have further questions or need guidance.

- Offer your support: Be willing to help them in return, such as providing information or referrals.

- Attend industry events together: Strengthen your bond through shared experiences.

Maintain Open Communication

- Check in periodically: Send a brief email or text to see how they're doing.

- Be a good listener: Show genuine interest in their career and personal life.

- Respect their time: Avoid being overly demanding or time-consuming.

Cultivate a Long-Term Relationship

- Be patient: Building strong relationships takes time.

- Focus on mutual respect: Treat the person with kindness and professionalism.

- Offer value: Continuously demonstrate your worth as a connection.

Remember, the goal is to build a genuine relationship based on mutual respect and shared interests. By following these steps, you can nurture your informational interview connections into valuable professional alliances.

Of course, conducting informational interviews is only the beginning of building relationships and connections. In reality, life is about connections, and nobody achieves what they achieve solely on their own merits. There is always someone behind the scenes who is working on their behalf so they can elevate to the next level. Sadly, there will always be people on the opposite side, or what I call "playa haters," who will try to dig holes for you to fall in. You cannot stop anyone from not liking or being jealous of you, but I advise you not to allow yourself to be manipulated by them, because I believe in karma. I think it's always good practice to simply treat people the way you want to be treated and remain open to possible opportunities for your personal and professional growth.

Networking & Elevator Pitch

Networking is an art because it involves presenting yourself to the right people at the right moment and in the right setting. One way of introducing yourself, making your point and establishing a connection is called an elevator pitch. It's called this because it should take about thirty seconds. It's designed to generate interest and initiate conversation. It should convey your value or the benefits you can offer that person or organization, but it should sound natural and be persuasive. Practice it often so it feels as easy as saying your name. Keep it concise, engaging, and memorable. Keep this in your head so you're always prepared because you never know when you'll meet someone who could make a difference in your life. If you have business cards, carry them with you to hand out as you make your pitch. Your elevator speech should include the following:

- Who are you? Briefly introduce yourself and your background.

- What do you do? Clearly state your profession, role, or what you are seeking.

- What value do you offer? Explain the benefits of your services or products.

- What's next? End with a strong call to action.

You must consistently network and stay connected to develop and build on your personal and professional growth. Research industry publications and attend relevant events to learn more about opportunities and connect with like-minded individuals. When attending events, be sure to bring your business cards.

With today's technology, you can have a digital business card on your smartphone. Some must-haves for a networking event are:

- Business cards: This is a must-have for exchanging contact information. There are both actual cards and digital business cards.

- Pen: For taking notes on business cards or jotting down important information.

- Smartphone: This is for connecting with new contacts, looking up information, and taking photos (if allowed).

Optional but Helpful to Carry:

- Breath mints: Fresh breath is always appreciated.

- Notebook or notepad: For taking more detailed notes.

- Portfolio: If you have physical samples of your work to share.

To get into a career or start a business requires that you do the work by networking and connecting with the right people and events and conducting informational interviews. This process is not a sprint but a marathon. Always have a positive attitude, be honest, and communicate with those you need to speak with. Getting to where you want and need to be is a process that takes being strategic and making an effort. The key is never to give up and to maintain your focus at all times.

Chapter 9: Your Crew Matters

Choosing Wisely

Choosing your friends and the people you hang out with depends on many factors. When I was growing up, many of my friends were from my neighborhood. We had a lot in common because so often the only thing we wanted to do was laugh and joke, play sports, and have fun. Life was good because we were insulated in a neighborhood with adults who looked after us and would also put us in our place if we got out of line. Naturally, when I went away to college, my circle of friends expanded because I met new people and joined new groups. That didn't mean I turned my back on my buddies from my neighborhood, though, because when I went home during summer and school breaks, we would pick up where we'd left off - laughing and joking around.

The first summer I came home, I felt much older. While I'd drunk a little beer in high school, that wasn't my thing back then. But when I went to college, I developed a drinking habit, as I mentioned earlier, so during my school breaks, I would hang out on the corner and drink with my friends. We would talk about women and anything else our egos allowed. One night, while hanging out, one of my friends ran across some ladies he knew. They invited him back to one of their homes, and he asked if I wanted to come along. Naturally, I said, "Yeah, man!" There we were with two young ladies, and who knew what would happen? So we went to their place, and while we were chatting, my friend pulled out a crack pipe. My buddy and both of the women started smoking. I will never forget that awful smell. It was as disgusting as the smell of something that had been dead for a while. He asked me, "Al, do you want some?" And at that moment, a little voice told me, *You better not touch it!* So, I answered, "Hell, no, I don't want that shit!" After I left, I realized what had just happened and was thankful that I hadn't fallen prey to that crack. I know that it was my guardian angel who told me not to do it, even while I was intoxicated and in a weak state to make good decisions.

That experience opened my eyes on a couple of fronts. First, I realized I could not put myself in positions where what I stand for could be compromised. Second, while those were my childhood friends, I knew I had to distance myself from them; though I would never turn my back on them, because we would be friends for life. But I had to decide when and where to hang out with them. I knew that I had to change some of my habits, and instead of looking down on my boys, I had to become more of an encourager to them. I knew about the crack epidemic. It was running rampant throughout many communities. My friends respected me, and even to this day, they know where I stand on things. But they also know I love them like a brother and want the best for them even when we stumble. That was not the last time I had a run-in with someone doing drugs in my company, but I made it very clear where I stood and disassociated myself from them.

Choosing your friends, or the crew you hang around, is vital to your life direction. When we're growing up, most kids tend to gel together because you all do a lot of the same things that kids typically do. But as we get older, there comes a time when we might have to separate ourselves from the friends we grew up with because we each develop different habits and interests. I have even grown apart from some of my relatives because our interests have changed as we've grown older.

The Power of Friendship

We all long for friendship because we want to be accepted and feel like we belong. This is sometimes the reason kids join gangs: to have that sense of belonging and appreciation. Some friendships last only a season, while others last a lifetime. Some create positive energy, while others stoke negativity. Regardless, friendships are a powerful force that helps us bond together.

As I matured, I understood better that friends might be there only a season while others are there for a lifetime. That is not a slight on my friends, but an acceptance of where we have been or might want to go. My boys from the neighborhood will always be my friends because we share the memories of growing up, playing, and joking around. Even to this day, we reminisce about those times. I have also developed a better understanding of what and who true friends are because true friends can help you grow and develop as an individual. They challenge you to think critically, broaden your perspectives, and step outside of your comfort zone. They support you through difficult times and provide an outlet to vent your frustrations.

Not all friendships are equal, of course. There may be times when you will have to back away from some friendships. I have shared things with friends that I would not tell others. I communicate with some friends for mutual interests, while others are built on trust, respect, and genuine care. Regardless of our level of friendship, my approach and foundation are centered on treating all of my friends the way I want to be treated. This means:

- Being a good friend. In other words, be reliable, trustworthy, and supportive.

- Communicating openly and honestly. Share your feelings, thoughts, and experiences with your friends. Be willing to share both the good and the bad.

- Checking up on them. Be thoughtful by checking up on your friends to ensure they are in a good space.

- Respecting each other's boundaries. Everyone has their limits and needs. Be mindful of your friends' boundaries and respect their wishes.

- Forgiving and forgetting. Everyone makes mistakes. If your friend does something wrong, try to forgive them and move on. Holding grudges can damage friendships.

Remember, friendships are a valuable gift and a two-way street. I'm not suggesting you do things with the expectation of a return, but that you understand the dynamics of your friendships. Cherish the ones you have and stay open to forming new ones. Friendships can enrich your life in countless ways, so make the most of them.

Understanding Yourself and What You Stand For

As I was growing up, I encountered several situations that challenged my integrity and made me question whether to do what was right. Those encounters were natural because, as a boy, I was explorative, or as my mother said, I was always into something. Mom was right because I always wanted to see how things worked or did not listen. For instance, at a family reunion, my mother told me not to go down to the river. Did I listen? Of course not, I went anyway. While playing with my cousin, I walked into a mud hole, and the mud came up to my waist. Thankfully, my other cousins were able to find a branch and pull me out. My mother was terrified because, again, that was a moment where I could have died. As a kid, I was obviously driven by the desire to do what I wanted to do. I did not consider consequences or dangers. These two incidents, however, scared me very much because I understood that I could have been hurt or, even worse, killed. Those events led me to want to be safe and do the right thing by listening to my parents and being mindful of my actions. It became clear to me early on that my actions had consequences.

Hanging out with my neighborhood friends was always an eventful experience. We would do some bad things, but nothing that was against the law, and I am thankful that we never crossed that line. That doesn't mean that we didn't do silly things that would get us in trouble with our parents, but because of what I had previously experienced, my mind was set on doing what would keep me safe and protected. I knew there were things that would cross the line, and my friends knew what I stood for. I was not afraid to share my thoughts and how I felt. Like boys, they would laugh and poke fun at me, but to this day, they all respect me because they know I wanted the best for them and myself. I haven't told them, but the truth is that I still maintain some guiding principles. They are:

- Honor my mother and father and respect adults.

- Treat others the way I want to be treated.

- Do not steal and be truthful.

- Work hard as well as work smart.

It wasn't as if I was a goodie two-shoes, but I held firm to my ideals while still being cool with my friends. So, how do you maintain your identity while being cool with your friends?

Your Elevation Determines Who You Hang Out With

Most of us have heard the saying, "Birds of a feather flock together." In other words, your crew and the people you spend your time with are usually people with similar interests who share your perspective about things, and they help shape who you are. Our friendships and relationships have a profound impact on who we become. The people we hang out with can shape our values, beliefs, and future goals.

Recognizing Good and Bad Influences

So, how do you know if the people you're hanging out with are good for you? Discovering this could happen over time or suddenly, and you may no longer be able to be in certain friendships. For example, a friend and I went out of town, and he rode with me in my car. After we arrived at our destination and had time to pay for our lodging, he told me he didn't have money but had some weed he could sell. That infuriated me, and I told him so. First, because he did not have the money to pay for the room, and second, and more importantly, he'd had drugs in my car. I told him he had better get the money to pay for half of the room, and I instantly decided we could no longer be friends. I did not do drugs, and I knew what type of trouble I could find myself in if I was caught with drugs in my car. I am not claiming to be a saint, but there were, and still are, some things I won't support, and drugs are at the top of my list.

I recognize that we are all different and have different motivations, but it's important to know which of the people you spend time with are genuine friends. Here are a few things to consider as you assess those relationships:

- Do your friends support your goals? True friends will encourage you to be the best version of yourself. They'll celebrate your successes and help you through tough times.

- Do they make you feel good about yourself? Healthy friendships should be uplifting. You shouldn't feel pressured to change who you are or to do things you don't want to do.

- Do they have positive influences in their own lives? The people you surround yourself with can have a significant impact on you. If they're making good choices, it's more likely that you'll make good choices, too.

If you're hanging out with people who are constantly getting into trouble, using drugs, or disrespecting others, those are red flags. They are not the kind of people who will help you reach your full potential. Unfortunately, recognizing these red flags might sometimes happen when we are already entrenched in the friendship, so, how do we break away?

Breaking Free from a Bad Influence: A Step-by-Step Guide

Recognizing that a friendship is no longer good for you can be difficult, but it's an important step toward personal growth. Here's a guide to help you break free:

1. Identify Toxic Behaviors

- Negative influences: Do they constantly bring you down or encourage harmful behaviors?

- Lack of support: Do they fail to support your goals or celebrate your achievements?

- Manipulation: Do they try to control your actions or emotions?

- Constant drama: Do they create unnecessary conflict or drama?

2. Prioritize Your Well-being

- Self-care: Focus on activities that bring you joy and help you relax.

- Set boundaries: Communicate your needs and limits to the toxic friend.

- Seek support: Talk to a trusted friend, family member, or therapist about your situation.

3. Communicate Your Concerns

- Choose a safe space: Find a time and place for a private conversation with the friend in question.

- Be honest and direct: Express your feelings and concerns in a calm and respectful manner.

- Listen actively: Be open to hearing their perspective, but don't let them manipulate the situation.

4. Limit Contact

- Gradual distancing: Start by spending less time together.

- Set clear boundaries: Be firm in your decision to limit contact.

- Avoid confrontations: Try to avoid arguments or heated discussions.

5. Focus on Positive Relationships

- Nurture healthy friendships: Spend time with people who uplift and support you.

- Join new groups or activities: Meet new people who share your interests.

- Seek professional help: If you're struggling to cope with the end of a friendship, consider talking to a therapist.

Remember, breaking free from a toxic friendship can be challenging, but it's a necessary step toward personal growth and happiness. Prioritize your well-being and surround yourself with positive influences.

When we're young and even as adults, we all want to be a part of something that gives us a sense of belonging and togetherness. This is a natural feeling because we all need affirmation. This is why some young guys join gangs, and I understand that. By no means am I condoning their behavior, but when we know the reasons, we can see that it often stems from something they lack at home. The fact is, street gangs existed even in Ancient Rome and Medieval Europe, and over time, spread throughout the globe. As cities grew in the United States, gangs began to form, particularly in New York and Chicago. Many gangs were often based on ethnicity or neighborhood.

Why People Join Gangs

The reasons why boys join gangs are complex and multilayered, but here are some common factors:

- Sense of Belonging: Many boys feel isolated or excluded from mainstream society. Gangs offer a sense of belonging and camaraderie.

- Protection: Gangs can provide a sense of security in dangerous neighborhoods. Members may feel safer when they are part of a group.

- Status and Power: Gangs often engage in activities that confer status and power within a community.

- Economic Opportunity: In many cases, gangs provide income opportunities, though these are usually through illegal means.

- Peer Pressure: The influence of friends and family can be a significant factor in joining a gang.

Of course, it's important to note that these are generalizations, and individual experiences may vary. Additionally, the reasons for joining a gang can change over time.

The Dangers of Street Gangs

One of the most dangerous situations a young man can find himself in is joining a gang. Gangs often involve violence, crime, and illegal activities. Joining a gang can have serious consequences, including:

- Legal trouble: Gang members are more likely to be arrested and convicted of crimes.

- Violence: Gangs are often involved in violent confrontations with rival gangs.

- Injury or death: Gang violence can lead to serious injuries or even death.

- Limited opportunities: Being a gang member can make getting a job, going to college, or building a successful future extremely difficult.

Getting Out of a Gang

It can be difficult to leave a gang once you are a member, but there is hope. Here are a few things you can do:

- Reach out for help: Talk to a trusted adult, like a parent, teacher, or counselor. They can provide support and guidance.

- Join a positive group: Get involved in activities that are healthy and constructive, like sports, clubs, or community service.

- Develop new friendships: Surround yourself with positive people who will encourage you to make good choices.

- Seek professional help: If you're struggling to cope with the consequences of leaving a gang, consider talking to a therapist or counselor.

Why associate with someone who steals when you hope to become a lawyer one day? Why engage in violent behavior that harms others when you dream of becoming a doctor? You need to be strong and know what you stand for, which comes from understanding yourself. Knowing your strengths, weaknesses, values, and goals is key to choosing the right friends. By recognizing what makes you unique, you can find people who complement your personality and ambitions. Just remember, true friendship is a two-way street, and being a supportive and uplifting friend in return will ensure your friendship lasts a lifetime.

By choosing positive and supportive friends who align with our values and goals, we can unlock our full potential and achieve our dreams. When I was young, I knew plenty of people who drank and did drugs. But because I was raised well and taught right from wrong, their behaviors did not influence my decision-making or value system. I also believe that by a certain age, we inherently know right from wrong. If we try to steal something from a store, for example, we try to hide it or make a run for it because we know it's wrong. Once, when I was a child, I wanted some cheese popcorn in a store, so I took the bag and walked out. When I arrived at my cousin's house, he noticed I had taken it without paying. He was upset and scolded me, and then he went back to the store to pay for it. I was too young to know it was wrong, so I had simply carried the bag out of the store without trying to hide it, but from that point on, I knew it was stealing, and that stealing was wrong.

Depending on where you live, it might be more difficult for you to stay away from negative influences than it is for people living in different neighborhoods. But if you desire a successful and happy life, make the effort. If negative influences surround you, try to distance yourself from any toxic friendships and seek new connections with like-minded people. Join clubs, volunteer, or participate in activities that align with your interests. Expanding your social circle will allow you to meet positive and inspiring people who can support your growth and help you achieve your goals.

Chapter 10: Level Up Your Relationships

The Power of Respect

As I've alluded to many times now, I was always taught to treat others the way I want to be treated - with respect and fairness. This core principle of how to treat others is practiced through self-awareness and consistent effort. It's not simply a passive idea but an active practice that demands mindful attention to our actions, words, and nonverbal cues. Our behavior serves as an internal guide, leading us toward honorable and respectful conduct, regardless of external circumstances. We must respect ourselves to build strong, lasting friendships and relationships. Respect is not just about politeness but is the foundation for trust, understanding, and genuine connection. When you treat others with respect, you're saying, "I value you, your thoughts, and your feelings." This simple act opens doors to deeper conversations, stronger bonds, and a more positive environment for everyone. It's the ultimate relationship superpower, and you can start developing it right now.

What Exactly Is Respect?

Let's clarify what we mean by respect. Respect isn't about fear or always agreeing with someone; it's about mutual understanding. True respect isn't about feeling intimidated or simply nodding along with everything someone says. Instead, it's about recognizing the inherent worth of yourself or another person, even if you strongly disagree with them. For example, I recently spoke with my son, Hilton, about navigating life. I told him that he would encounter people along the way who would try to disrespect him but that he should always stand up for himself. I also shared a story from my own work experience years ago. My supervisor would often say, "You go, boy!" whenever I closed a deal or did well. I found that deeply offensive because I am not a boy. He said it a few times, and I asked to speak with him privately. I explained that I found that phrase offensive. He listened and immediately apologized, and that was the last time he said it to me. I also explained to my son that respecting yourself by standing up for yourself doesn't mean cursing someone out or starting a fight. It means using your head, letting people know how you feel, and teaching them how to treat you.

When you respect yourself, you're better positioned to value others' thoughts, feelings, and boundaries, recognizing that they're individuals with their own experiences and perspectives, just like you. This includes giving them space to express themselves, listening without interruption, and acknowledging their right to their own opinions, even if they differ from your own. When you show respect, it's not just a gift to the other person; it's a gift to yourself. It enhances your self-worth, attracts better people into your life, and fosters a positive environment around you. Plus, when you respect others, they are far more likely to respect you in return. It's a win-win.

The Starting Line: Respecting Yourself First

You can't truly respect others if you don't respect yourself. You have to recognize your worth, establish personal boundaries, and prevent others from taking advantage of you. Self-respect isn't selfish but rather, it is vital for healthy relationships.

Recognizing Your Worth

I'm not talking about being arrogant or feeling superior to anyone else, just recognizing that you have inherent value as an individual. You also possess unique strengths, talents, and perspectives. For example, if friends regularly seek your advice, you might realize you're an excellent problem-solver, or if you stick with a tough video game level until you beat it, you're persistent when you're determined to accomplish something. Acknowledge these qualities!

Take an honest look in the mirror and ask yourself, "What am I good at?" Maybe there are things you're great at, but maybe you're also currently working to become better at something, so you're making progress. All this reflects your purpose and who you are as a person. Below are steps to help you recognize your worth.

Steps to recognize your worth:

1. Self-Reflection: Take time to think about what you're good at, what you've achieved (big or small), and what positive qualities you possess. Are you a loyal friend? A quick learner? A good listener? Write them down.

2. Accept Imperfections: Nobody's perfect. Recognizing your worth also means accepting your flaws and understanding they don't diminish your value as a person.

3. Positive Self-Talk: Challenge negative thoughts about yourself. Instead

of "I'm so bad at this," try "I'm still learning, and I'll get better."

Establishing Personal Boundaries

Boundaries are like invisible lines in relationships that set what is acceptable and what isn't. They protect your time, energy, emotions, and values. This is very important because the people you associate with can either add value to your life positively or negatively. If you know your worth and don't worry about peer pressure, you'll find it easier to set personal boundaries. For example, if a friend constantly asks to copy your homework, a boundary could be: "I can help you understand the concepts, but I won't let you copy my work, because that's cheating." Below are steps to help you establish boundaries.

Steps to establish boundaries:

1. Identify Your Needs: What makes you feel uncomfortable, drained, or disrespected? Do you need alone time after school? Do you dislike being interrupted?

2. Communicate Clearly: Once you know your boundaries, express them calmly and directly. Use "I" statements: "I need some quiet time to focus on my homework," or "I'm not comfortable talking about that."

3. Be Consistent: The first time you set a boundary, someone might test it. Stick to your guns. Consistency teaches others how to treat you.

Preventing Others from Taking Advantage of You:

When you have self-respect and clear boundaries, you'll become more aware of when others are trying to take advantage of you. When you value yourself, you're less likely to let others exploit your kindness or generosity. This doesn't mean you shouldn't give or understand others; it means you need to evaluate the situation and consider others' motives. For example, if a friend always conveniently "forgets" their wallet when you go out, and you end up paying for them, you might say, "Hey, I'm happy to hang out, but I can't cover your share tonight." Below are steps to help you prevent others from taking advantage of you.

Steps to prevent being taken advantage of:

1. Learn to Say "No": "No" is a complete sentence. You don't always need an elaborate excuse. "No, I can't do that right now" is perfectly fine.

2. Recognize Red Flags: Pay attention if someone only contacts you when they need something, consistently asks for favors without reciprocating, or dismisses your feelings.

3. Prioritize Your Well-being: Your time, energy, and emotional health are valuable. Don't continually sacrifice them for others, especially if they don't show you the same consideration.

Self-respect isn't selfish; it's the bedrock upon which all healthy interactions are built. When you respect yourself, you're showing others how to respect you, too.

Showing Up: Practical Ways to Show Respect to Others

So how do you show respect to others? This is where we get practical. Showing respect is an active verb, something you do rather than just say. For starters, one way to show respect is to look people in the eye and give them your full attention when they are speaking. This shows you're engaged and that what they're saying matters. Active listening (really hearing what someone says, not just waiting for your turn to talk) is also key. Instead of planning your response while someone is talking, focus on understanding their message, and then summarize it back to them to confirm you understood: "So, if I'm hearing you correctly, you're feeling frustrated because..." Showing empathy (trying to understand their perspective) means putting yourself in their shoes. If a friend is upset about a bad grade, even if it doesn't seem like a big deal to you, you might say, "I get why you're feeling down about that; it's tough when you put in effort and don't see the results you hoped for."

Respecting boundaries (both yours and theirs) is crucial. If a friend tells you they need space, respect that by giving them room. Similarly, if you've set a boundary about not lending money, for example, stick to it even if it feels awkward. Keeping your word builds trust; if you say you'll be somewhere at a particular time or that you'll do something, follow through. If you promise to help a buddy move, show up and do your part. Finally, communicating honestly but kindly means speaking your truth without being rude or aggressive. If you need to give feedback, phrase it constructively: "I appreciate you asking for my opinion, and I think we could improve this by trying things this way." These actions, big and small, send a clear message: "I respect you."

Respect in Action: Different Relationships, Different Nuances

Respect varies depending on the person with whom you're interacting, and showing respect is essential for building strong relationships. The truth is that everyone needs someone to support them along their life's journey, and I can't think of anyone who has succeeded alone. Understanding, finding common ground, and nurturing the relationship are all elements of respect. While all healthy relationships are based on respect, they differ in other ways.

Family: Our family relationships are usually the first ones we experience, and they can be complex. Respect in these relationships involves listening to parents and guardians, even when we disagree, and appreciating their efforts to provide for us and guide us. Respect also means being patient with siblings, understanding that they're on their own path and sometimes need space or support. For instance, if your parents ask you to do a chore, respecting them means doing it without argument, even if you'd rather be doing something else. Or, if your younger sibling is bothering you, showing respect might mean taking a deep breath and walking away instead of lashing out. This behavior cultivates understanding and strengthens the core bonds of your life.

Friends: These are the people we choose to share our life with, in other words, our chosen family. Respect here means loyalty—standing by them even when things get tough—and honesty, even when something is hard to hear or say. Don't talk behind their back—if you have an issue, address it directly or keep it to yourself. For example, if a friend tells you something confidentially, keep their secret, even if others pressure you to share it. It also means genuinely celebrating their successes and offering a listening ear without judgment when they're struggling. Doing these things helps build a deeper connection and trust between you and your friends.

Romantic Relationships: These relationships often involve a higher level of vulnerability and closeness. Respect is essential, and encompasses trust, reliability, transparency, and open communication, where both partners feel safe to share their true selves. Importantly, it includes respecting "no," whether that's about physical boundaries, emotional availability, or simply not wanting to do something. We must value their feelings and autonomy and recognize that their needs and desires are just as important as ours. For example, if your partner says they're not ready for a certain step in your relationship, respecting them means accepting that without pressuring them or making them feel guilty.

Teachers and Authority Figures: While these relationships aren't about deep personal connections, respect still plays a central role. Listen when they speak, follow rules intended for everyone's benefit, and interact respectfully even if you disagree with them. You can share a different opinion or ask clarifying questions without being rude or dismissive. For example, if you think a teacher's assignment is unfair, respecting them involves calmly talking to them after class to share your concerns instead of complaining loudly during class or ignoring the assignment. This approach helps create a positive environment for learning and growth.

Professional Colleagues: As we move into the working world, respecting our colleagues becomes a requirement for creating a productive environment. Collaborating effectively, sharing the workload fairly, and acknowledging others' contributions are all part of respecting co-workers. Professional communication means being clear and concise in emails and meetings, and honoring deadlines that affect others' work. Even if you don't always agree with a colleague's approach, respecting them means listening to their ideas and finding common ground. For example, if you're working on a group project, it's important to pull your weight, be on time for meetings, and communicate any delays promptly. We also must make sure we give credit where credit is due and offer constructive feedback rather than criticism. These behaviors build a strong sense of teamwork and mutual understanding.

Online Interactions: In today's world, many of our interactions happen online. The importance of digital respect cannot be overstated. Cyberbullying, negativity, and spreading rumors are all bad behaviors that should be avoided, and we must all think before we post or comment on anything. Remember, there's a real person with real feelings behind every screen name. Suppose, for example, that you see someone has posted something you disagree with. Respecting them means either scrolling past or engaging in a polite, constructive debate, rather than resorting to insults or personal attacks. Online spaces should be places of connection, not conflict, but these days we're getting further and further away from that ideal.

When Respect Is Missing: Dealing with Disrespect

Not everyone will treat you with respect; some relationships that start strong might not last, and that's a harsh truth. How do you handle it when you feel disrespected or when you notice the relationship has devolved to a level where you are not comfortable continuing? Below are steps that will empower you to identify disrespect, set clear boundaries (and stick to them), and know when it's time to walk away from relationships that are consistently unhealthy or diminishing. Remember, your self-respect demands it.

Identifying Disrespect: Disrespect isn't always obvious. Sometimes it's a subtle jab, a dismissive tone, or a pattern of ignoring your needs. Learning to recognize these signs is the first step.

Signs of Disrespect:

- Dismissing your feelings: "You're overreacting." "It's not a big deal."

- Ignoring your boundaries: Continuously pushing you to do things you've said no to.

- Constant interruptions or not listening: Talking over you, changing the subject, or looking at their phone when you're speaking.

- Belittling or mocking: Making fun of your ideas, dreams, or appearance.

- Breaking promises repeatedly: Showing they don't value your time or trust.

- Talking behind your back: Spreading rumors or negative gossip.

- Taking advantage of your kindness: Always asking for favors without reciprocating.

Below are various scenarios and corresponding strategies to handle them in different relationship contexts.

Friends:

Scenario: A friend constantly makes jokes at your expense in front of others, even after you've told them it bothers you. They might say, "Lighten up, it's just a joke!"

Solution: After clearly communicating your boundary ("I don't like it when you make fun of me, even if you think it's a joke"), if the behavior persists, you might need to limit your time with them or even end the friendship.

Example of Action: "Look, I've told you this makes me uncomfortable. If you can't respect that, I don't think we can hang out as much anymore." Or you might start declining invitations without making a dramatic announcement.

Romantic Relationships:

Scenario: Your partner frequently dismisses your feelings during arguments, saying things like, "You're being too sensitive," or makes decisions that affect both of you without consulting you.

Solution: This is a critical area for self-respect. After attempting open and honest communication about how their actions impact you, if the pattern of disrespect continues, it's a sign the relationship isn't healthy.

Example of Action: "When you say I'm too sensitive, it makes me feel like my feelings don't matter to you. I need a partner who respects my emotions. If we can't work through this, I need to reconsider our future together." This might lead to couples counseling or, if things don't improve, ending the relationship.

Professional Colleagues:

Scenario: A colleague consistently takes credit for your ideas in meetings or frequently undermines your contributions to a team project.

Solution: First, address it directly and professionally. If that doesn't work, consider escalating the issue to a manager or HR. If the environment remains toxic and impacts your well-being or career progression, seeking a new opportunity might be the best solution.

Example of Action: "John, you presented my idea about the new technology rollout as your own in the meeting earlier. I'd appreciate it if you'd acknowledge my contributions in the future." If the behavior continues, you might say, "I've tried to address this with you directly, but you haven't listened to my concerns. I'm going to have to bring this to [Management/Human Resources]."

Online Interactions:

Scenario: You're part of an online gaming community, and a few members constantly send you abusive messages or make personal attacks.

Solution: The beauty of online spaces is often the "block" and "report" features. Don't engage with trolls. If it's a platform you value, report the behavior to the administrators. If the platform itself is consistently toxic, it might be time to find a new community.

Example of Action: Immediately block the user. If it's a group chat or forum, report the messages to the moderator. If the harassment is severe, consider taking screenshots as evidence, but refrain from engaging in a back-and-forth argument; it only fuels their behavior and your own frustration.

Ultimately, the power of respect is a key tool in your relationship toolkit. It begins with understanding and cultivating self-respect, which then enables you to show genuine respect to others in all areas of your life—from your closest friends and family to your professional colleagues and online connections. While relationships can be challenging, especially when disrespect occurs, remember that you have the ability to recognize these moments, set clear boundaries, and, when necessary, walk away from situations that diminish your worth. By consistently applying these principles, you're not only building stronger, healthier relationships; you're actively creating a life filled with trust, understanding, and mutual respect.

I urge you to embrace the process of building respect, both for yourself and those around you. It's an ongoing process of learning, growing, and yes, sometimes even letting go. But with each step, you'll find yourself surrounded by more genuine connections, a deeper sense of self-worth, and the profound satisfaction of truly improving your relationships and, by extension, your entire life.

Chapter 11: Planning Your Future

A Blueprint for Greatness

I remember having big dreams while growing up—dreams of playing a guitar in a famous band or being a fighter pilot. My mind would run wild just thinking about what I wanted to do. The beauty of being young is that we can let our minds run free as we dream of the things we want to become. In my dream, I had no boundaries to what I could do because as a kid, if there was something I wanted to do, I would find a way to do it. But some things were more important to me, so I might've focused more on them and less on other things that I should have.

As I've said, being a football and track star in high school was very important to me, so I dedicated myself to practicing and improving in those sports. Did

I work as hard as possible on my schoolwork? No. I worked to get satisfactory grades, mainly because my parents expected me to do well academically. So, I did well enough in high school to go on to college. In college, I maintained a GPA between 2.5 and 2.75, which was just okay. But when I decided to pursue graduate school, I finally started giving my maximum effort. Looking back, while I am thankful to have graduated from college and earned graduate degrees, I wish I had put more effort into my undergraduate studies, because that could have opened more doors of opportunity for me. I don't dwell on regret, though, and instead think of it as a learning experience. And as a result, I've told my children to always do their best in school, because good grades can open some doors, but excellent grades can open many more doors.

When we are young, our decision-making and focus might not be at the same level as adults, but that doesn't mean we can't know where we want to go and how to get there. We just need to plan for the future. This includes self-reflection, setting goals, creating a plan, taking action, and remaining flexible.

Self-Reflection

Self-reflection involves examining one's thoughts, feelings, and behaviors. It's like stepping back and viewing yourself from a different angle. Self-reflection is helpful at any age; I still do it today. I do it to see if I handle situations appropriately or say things correctly. I don't always get it right, even at my age, which is why I sometimes call someone back to clarify what I said or to apologize. Self-reflection can also reveal others' intentions, and you may need to reach out to clarify or understand them better.

Incorporating self-reflection into your life can be invaluable. It can bring balance because it pushes you to consider all sides of a situation, question, or cause. I recall taking a systems class while pursuing my MBA. In that class, we explored various scenarios called systems thinking. One process we used was if-then statements, which are simple cause-and-effect relationships that show how one event or condition leads to another. If-then statements can be both positive and negative. For example, if you consistently eat a balanced diet and exercise regularly, then you will likely experience improved physical health and increased energy. That yields positive results. On the other hand, if you consistently neglect your responsibilities, then you will fail to achieve your long-term goals. This method can be applied to various situations, bringing clarity and precision, and it can serve as a powerful tool for self-reflection and future planning. Here's how:

Identifies how situations intersect: We are part of complex systems influenced by factors like family, friends, education, and societal structures. Systems thinking helps us recognize these connections and how they impact our choices and outcomes.

Shows how choices create an effect: Our actions create positive and negative results. Understanding how our choices impact us allows us to see how they ripple through our lives so we can adjust our course accordingly.

Offers long-term perspective: Systems thinking encourages us to think beyond immediate consequences. It helps us consider the long-term implications of our decisions and how they might affect our future goals.

Self-Awareness

Self-reflection also leads us to self-awareness, allowing us to do a SWOT analysis on ourselves. This is basically a way to identify our strengths, weaknesses, opportunities, and threats (SWOT). By examining your thoughts, feelings, and behaviors, you can gain valuable insights into your current situation and future potential.

Here's how self-reflection can help you identify each element of a SWOT analysis:

Strengths:

Positive Attributes: Self-reflection allows you to recognize your positive qualities, such as your skills, talents, and personality traits.

Unique Abilities: By examining your past experiences, you can identify unique abilities that set you apart from others.

Weaknesses:

Areas for Improvement: Self-reflection helps you identify areas where you may need to develop or improve. This could include specific skills, knowledge, or habits.

Self-Limiting Beliefs: Examining your thoughts and beliefs can uncover any negative or limiting beliefs that may be holding you back.

Opportunities:

Potential Paths: Self-reflection can help you identify new opportunities, such as career advancements, educational pursuits, or personal projects.

External Factors: By examining external factors like industry trends, economic conditions, and technological advancements, you can identify career opportunities for yourself.

Threats:

Potential Obstacles: Self-reflection can help you identify obstacles or challenges that may hinder your progress. This could include financial constraints, time limitations, or health issues.

External Risks: Consider researching factors like competition, economic downturns, or political instability to identify potential threats to your career goals.

By conducting a thorough SWOT analysis of yourself, you can gain a deeper understanding of your strengths, weaknesses, opportunities, and threats. This valuable information can then be used to set goals, develop strategies, and make informed decisions to help you achieve your full potential.

Personal Growth

Reflecting on your experiences can help you identify areas for improvement and set personal development goals. Personal growth is an ongoing process of self-improvement and development. It involves expanding one's knowledge, skills, and understanding of oneself and the world. This often includes setting goals, learning new things, overcoming obstacles, and reflecting on experiences to foster personal and professional growth. We all view our own personal growth through a different lens: maybe it's to lose weight, maybe to get in better shape, become a better communicator, learn a new skill, live a healthier lifestyle or something else. Regardless of what it entails for you, analyzing personal growth is essential to do the following:

Bring about self-awareness: It helps us understand our strengths, weaknesses, values, and beliefs, leading to greater self-understanding.

Helps us set goals: By reflecting on past experiences and current progress, we can set realistic and meaningful goals for the future.

Fosters skill development: Analyzing personal growth allows us to identify areas for improvement and develop new skills.

It shifts our mindset: It encourages a growth mindset, fostering a belief in our ability to learn and grow, even in the face of challenges.

It increases our motivation: Tracking progress and celebrating achievements can boost motivation and drive for continued personal development.

Here are some ways a man can monitor and track his personal development:

Journaling: Regularly writing about thoughts, feelings, experiences, and goals can provide valuable insights and help track progress.

Goal-setting and tracking: Setting specific, measurable, achievable, relevant, and time-bound (SMART) goals and regularly tracking progress can help maintain focus and motivation.

Self-reflection: Regular self-reflection, such as meditation or mindfulness exercises, can help you gain deeper insights into yourself and your growth.

Seeking feedback from mentors, colleagues, or friends can provide valuable external perspectives on your strengths and areas for improvement.

Skill assessments: Taking online courses, attending workshops, or seeking professional assessments can help identify skill gaps and track progress in skill development.

Personal development plans: Creating a personalized development plan outlining specific goals, action steps, and timelines can provide a structured approach to personal growth.

Personal growth is a lifelong process, and there is no one-size-fits-all approach. The key is to find what works best for you and to be consistent in your efforts to develop and improve yourself.

Improved Relationships

Understanding yourself better helps you communicate more effectively and build stronger relationships with others. Self-reflection can also help you manage stress by identifying and addressing negative thought patterns. It is a powerful tool for fostering personal growth and enhancing well-being. It empowers you to take control of your life and make positive changes. Here are five steps you can follow to help you better understand yourself and your life goals.

Determine Who You Are:

Identify Your Passions: What truly excites you? What activities make you lose track of time?

Assess Your Strengths and Weaknesses: Understand what you're good at and where you need improvement.

Define Your Values: What principles guide your life? Your values will influence your career and lifestyle choices.

Set Goals:

Short-Term Goals: These are smaller, achievable goals that help you progress towards your long-term vision.

Long-Term Goals: These are your big-picture goals, such as career aspirations, financial stability, or family plans.

Use the SMART Goal Framework: Make sure your goals are Specific, Measurable, Achievable, Relevant, and Time-bound.[2]

Create a Plan:

Education and Training: Find out what type of education or certifications you'll need to achieve your goals.

Career Path: Research potential career paths and industries that align with your interests and skills.

Financial Planning: Create a budget, set savings goals, and consider investments for your future.

Take Action:

Start Small: As mentioned above, break down your goals into smaller, manageable steps.

Build a Support Network: Surround yourself with positive and supportive people who will encourage you.

Stay Persistent: There will inevitably be obstacles along the way. Don't give up; keep pushing forward.

Be Flexible:

Adapt to Change: Life is unpredictable. Be open to new opportunities and be willing to adjust your plans.

Learn from Mistakes: Use setbacks as opportunities to learn and grow.

It's important to realize when we're young that our future is in our own hands. These steps will help you create a fulfilling and successful life, so may you use them in good health!

Building Your Blueprint

A blueprint is an outline or a plan of a design. It represents how something should or will look in the future. What is the blueprint for your life? Do you know? This is not about who your friends are, how much money you make, your job title or your academic achievements, but about your character and what you stand for - your core values. What type of image do you want to convey to others? In today's world, especially on social media and in the entertainment industry, too many are only presenting an image they want an audience to believe, rather than one that represents who they really are as a person. They are creating their own reality, not a genuine image of themselves, and too many young people are taken in by the fantasy.

We must be true to ourselves if we wish to be balanced, because when we're balanced, we're at peace with ourselves. Years ago, I often told friends to be true to themselves: to know who they are and live in their truth. When you're living your truth, you can look in the mirror with pride, joy, and understanding. When you understand who you are, what you stand for, and where you want to go, you will connect with your inner self. This is the beginning of developing your personal blueprint. Reflect on your past experiences, successes, failures, and unmet goals so you can nurture that all-important self-awareness. Ask yourself the why and how questions as you begin maturing into a man and growing educationally, financially, and socially. Below is a blueprint (of sorts) for you to follow in these three critical areas to ensure you're headed down the right path.

I. Educational Growth

Set Clear Goals: Define short-term and long-term educational objectives. This could include completing high school, pursuing a college degree, or acquiring specific vocational certifications.

Choose a Path: Research different educational options, including traditional college, online courses, apprenticeships, or vocational training programs. Consider your interests, career goals, and learning style.

Develop Strong Study Habits: Establish a consistent study routine, time management techniques, and effective note-taking strategies.

Seek Mentorship: Find a mentor or advisor who can offer guidance, support, and insights into your chosen field of study.

Embrace Lifelong Learning: Cultivate a curiosity for knowledge and a commitment to continuous learning.

II. Financial Growth

Financial Literacy: Develop a strong understanding of personal finance concepts, including budgeting, saving, investing, and debt management.

Create a Budget: Establish a realistic budget that tracks income and expenses and allows for savings and investment goals.

Start Saving: Begin saving early, even small amounts, and explore different savings vehicles like savings accounts, CDs, and even retirement plans.

Invest Wisely: Learn about different investment options, such as stocks, bonds, and mutual funds. Consider consulting with a financial advisor.

Build Creditworthiness: Establish and maintain a good credit score by paying bills on time, using credit responsibly, and avoiding excessive debt.

III. Social Growth

Build Strong Relationships: Invest time in nurturing meaningful relationships with family, friends, and mentors.

Develop Social Skills: Practice effective communication, active listening, empathy, and conflict resolution skills.

Join Social Groups and Clubs: Participate in activities and organizations that align with your interests and values.

Volunteer: Give back to your community through volunteering, which can also provide valuable networking opportunities.

Travel and Experience New Cultures: Broaden your horizons by exploring different cultures and perspectives.

Additional Elements to Consider in Your Blueprint

Physical Health: Prioritize physical fitness, nutrition, and regular exercise.

Mental Health: Practice self-care and stress management techniques and seek support when needed.

Ethical Development: Develop a strong moral compass and a commitment to ethical behavior.

Continuous Self-Improvement: Embrace a growth mindset and focus on personal development.

Of course, this is just a starting point, because your life and your needs will evolve as you gain experience and knowledge. Be adaptable, stay focused, and seek support from others as you navigate the path to becoming a well-rounded and successful man.

To help teens and young men get themselves on the right track, I have developed a 90-day plan. Focus and discipline are keys to staying on task and achieving your goals. Remember, you can accomplish anything with desire, faith, discipline, and focus. So, let's start today by becoming the best you can be for yourself, your family, and your community.

A 90-Day Blueprint for Personal Growth

Note: This is a general 90-day plan, so be sure to tailor it to your specific goals and circumstances.

Month 1: Foundation and Focus

- Weeks 1-2: Self-Assessment and Goal Setting

    - Reflect on your current situation by doing a SWOT analysis: strengths, weaknesses, opportunities, and threats.

    - Set SMART (Specific, Measurable, Achievable, Relevant,

Time-bound) goals for the next 90 days in education, finance, and social life.

  ○ Create a vision board to visualize your goals.

- Weeks 3-4: Educational Foundation

  ○ Research educational options: college, vocational training, online courses, etc.

  ○ Develop a study schedule: allocate specific time each day for studying and learning.

  ○ Start or join a study group to connect with like-minded individuals.

Month 2: Financial Fitness

- Weeks 5-6: Financial Literacy

  ○ Read books or take online courses on personal finance.

  ○ Create a budget: track income, expenses, and savings.

  ○ Set financial goals: short-term (e.g. emergency fund) and long-term (e.g. retirement).

- Weeks 7-8: Building Credit and Investing

  ○ Check your credit report and work on maintaining a good credit score or improving a bad one.

  ○ Start investing: Consider opening a brokerage account and investing in low-cost index funds.

  ○ Explore side hustle opportunities to increase your income.

Month 3: Social Growth and Wellness

- Weeks 9-10: Building Relationships

    ○ Reach out to friends and family: schedule regular check-ins.

    ○ Join social clubs or groups: network with people who share your interests.

    ○ Practice active listening and effective communication skills.

- Weeks 11-12: Physical and Mental Wellness

    ○ Create a workout routine and stick to it.

    ○ Practice mindfulness techniques like meditation or yoga.

    ○ Prioritize sleep and nutrition.

Additional Important Elements:

- Flexibility: Be flexible and adapt your plan as needed.

- Accountability: Track your progress and celebrate your achievements.

- Balance: Avoid burnout by balancing work, study, and leisure.

- Continuous Learning: Keep learning and growing, both personally and professionally.

This chapter has laid out a blueprint that you can begin using right away to reach your goals and plan a successful future. Remember, true greatness isn't a destination, but a continuous journey of intentional growth. We've explored how self-reflection, through tools like SWOT analysis, empowers you to understand your unique strengths and areas for improvement, setting the stage for meaningful goal-setting. By planning your educational, financial, and social development, and embracing the actionable steps outlined in my 90-day blueprint, you are not just dreaming of a better future – you are actively building it. Remember, flexibility, accountability, balance, and a commitment to continuous learning are your guiding stars. Your future is not just a distant concept; it's a masterpiece in the making, and with this blueprint in hand, you have the power to design an extraordinary life. You can do it!

Chapter 12: Elevate
A Final Word

I am a routine person. For example, I love waking up and making breakfast on Saturday mornings. During my preparation, I make phone calls. One person I always call is my brother, Ray. We have great conversations and talk about everything. I must admit that sometimes I frustrate him during our talks because I might slip in a joke or a one-liner. He usually pauses and says, "Alan, I am not going there with you today!" I laugh because I know I've temporarily thrown him off track. I do it to break the ice because we almost always end up talking about some serious things. Things like the world today, the Bible, and sports, but a frequent subject is community and its youth, especially young men. Ray knows I'm passionate about our community and the direction of young men. He also knows I believe a strong community relies on children having proper guidance and being prepared to succeed in society. And that boys need a parent, guardian, or mentor to teach them right from wrong and to be responsible. We often discuss the problems, but I like to focus on solutions.

As I've said several times now, I do understand that we all grow up in different circumstances. I know some youths come from extremely troubled homes, are homeless, or sometimes even have to raise themselves. These are serious situations that are hard to escape, but I believe in hope and that circumstances can improve if you take steps to change them. To make those changes, you must believe in yourself and seek support and guidance. You also need to develop a clear plan of who you want to become, where you want to go, and how you want others to see you. Building meaningful relationships is also essential to reaching your goals. Putting a plan into action is a good start, but what will give you the confidence to believe in yourself? For me, the answer is faith.

Believing in Yourself

When I first started playing football at twelve, I was drawn to it because I thought tackling looked fun; however, I didn't know anything about the game. When I went out there in equipment and the tackling began, I realized that seeing tackling on TV seemed fun but experiencing it in person was a whole different story. I was shy because I didn't want to get hurt. One day, during tackling drills, one of the coaches said, "Oh, Benson doesn't want to hit because he is a sissy." That angered me because I didn't want to be labeled as someone timid. The season ended, and I decided to return the following year, but I had to come to terms with what kind of football player I wanted to be, and to do that, I had to believe in myself.

When the next season rolled around, tackling drills came up, and I hit, tackled, and ran through my teammates. My coaches saw the change in me and excitedly congratulated me. More importantly, I congratulated myself because I had proved to myself that I belonged and that I was a football player.

That was one of many situations in life where I faced challenges, but I pushed through because I believed in myself. As my brother Ray would say, "It is all between your ears," meaning it's about what you think. You'll encounter situations that test your identity and determine if you have what it takes to persevere and succeed. So, when you find yourself facing a hurdle, follow the steps below to get through it. It's tough to conquer an obstacle when you're doubting yourself, so this is a breakdown of how to build that inner belief and confront any challenge head-on.

1. Recognize and Challenge Negative Thoughts: Identify the challenge and say to yourself, "I am capable," "I have overcome challenges before," "I am strong enough to handle this."

2. Focus on Your Strengths: Say, "I have made it this far and am strong enough for this new challenge."

3. Break Down the Challenge: Break the challenge into smaller, more manageable steps and celebrate small victories.

4. Visualize Your Winning: Imagine yourself overcoming the challenge and picture yourself conquering it!

5. Seek Support: Talk to someone you trust and find a role model. Don't be afraid to ask for help.

6. Take Care of Yourself: Prioritize your physical and mental health.

Believing in yourself is a trait that will have to be reinforced throughout your life. It requires time and effort, but by facing these challenges, you'll develop the stamina and wisdom to know which ones to pursue and which to step back from. Be patient with yourself, celebrate your progress, and never give up on your dreams! You can do it!

Having Support and Guidance

My son, Hilton, graduated with a degree in computer science and engineering, and is now working in his field and attending graduate school. I am incredibly proud of him and pray for his success in life. We talk often about his next career steps, and my approach when talking with him is to draw on my experiences and wisdom from those who have given me good advice. The one thing I have emphasized to my son is to develop relationships. Relationships are important in this society. They open doors, provide recommendations, and offer wise counsel. I first learned this when speaking to an administrator at the University of Louisville. I told this story earlier, but I think it bears repeating here. I asked him what opportunities would open for me if I earned a Master of Public Administration (MPA) degree. He said simply, "Having your MPA and not knowing anybody is like having only a quarter in your pocket." In other words, you must know people in this society if you have any hope of advancing in a career.

I have business relationships that span many years. The key to developing relationships is connecting with people who are going in your direction, both socially and professionally. Value all relationships regardless of who people are, of course, and don't burn any bridges by doing something to end the relationship because you never know when you might need that person. I do believe that relationships evolve and are sometimes heightened by opportunities. They might also become less important over time, but you should never close the door unless something drastic happens to end the relationship. Even if the relationship ends, always treat people the way you want to be treated.

If you are new to developing relationships, the suggestions below can help you create, nurture, and sustain meaningful connections.

I. Creating Meaningful Connections and Networks:

1. Silence your phone: You do not want distractions while meeting others, nor do you want to come off as rude.

2. Be genuine in your approach: Stand up straight and confidently. Look people in the eye while giving a firm handshake. Let them know who you are, i.e., graduating from school or seeking employment.

3. Pay attention while others speak: Listen closely to what others say, ask questions, and show genuine interest in their thoughts and perspectives.

4. Find common ground: Look for shared interests, values, or goals. Do they work at the place you are seeking employment?

5. Offer value: Consider what you can bring to the relationship. How can you help the other person? Share your expertise, resources, or connections.

6. Make a memorable impression: Be yourself, be enthusiastic, and follow up after the initial interaction to solidify the connection. Send them an email or even a personal note through the mail.

II. Nurturing and Sustaining the Relationship:

1. Don't be a stranger - stay in touch: Regular communication is key. Schedule check-ins, send occasional emails, like birthday wishes or holiday greetings, or make time for casual conversations.

2. Do what you say and be trustworthy: Follow through on your commitments, be punctual, and maintain confidentiality.

3. Show appreciation: Express gratitude for their time, support, and

contributions. A simple "thank you" goes a long way.

4. Provide support: Be there for them during difficult times, help when needed, and celebrate their successes. Don't wait to be asked for assistance; offer it.

5. Ask for feedback: Ask for their input and be willing to learn from their perspectives. This shows that you value their opinion.

III. Sustaining Long-Term Relationships:

1. Nurture the connection: Schedule face-to-face interactions, attend industry events together, or collaborate on projects.

2. Adapt to change: Be flexible and understanding as circumstances evolve. Adjust your communication style and support as needed.

3. Stay top-of-mind: Share relevant articles or resources, congratulate them on achievements, and remind them of important dates.

4. Rekindle fading connections: If you haven't spoken in a while, reach out and re-engage. A simple "checking in" can go a long way.

5. Always be professional: Maintain ethical behavior, respect boundaries, and avoid gossip or negativity.

Building strong business relationships takes time, effort, and commitment. It is not a race but rather a marathon in which you must be mindful of creating mutually beneficial connections based on trust and respect. Honesty, communication, reliability, and appreciation are prioritized to foster and sustain those relationships and will demonstrate your belief in the value of that relationship. Following these steps will help you create a network of meaningful business relationships that will contribute to your success and enrich your professional life.

Having Faith

Faith is the belief that something will be accomplished even when we cannot see it clearly. It is a mindset that trusts things will improve. For example, when we board a plane, we trust it will take us safely to our destination. We believe we will not have an accident when we get in our car to go to school or work. For many, faith is based on our connection to a higher power. For me, my faith is grounded in God and my spiritual background. Through my relationship with God and life experiences, I rely on Him for guidance and reassurance in everything I do; as far as I'm concerned, it will become a reality.

So, why is having faith important? Because it trains your mind to expect better outcomes. This influences you in countless ways. It affects your mental and emotional health and your ability to reach goals. It supports your overall mental well-being. Here are some ways faith contributes to our well-being.

IV. Mental and Emotional Well-being

Reduces Stress and Anxiety: Faith provides a sense of trust that things will eventually work out, even in difficult times. For example, when your car breaks down, and you don't know how to repair it, you believe it will be fixed. This comforts your mind and body, lowering levels of anxiety and depression.

Promotes Hope and Optimism: Faith fosters a belief in the possibility of positive change and a brighter future, which leads us to think positively. It's like getting a grade of C in a class; you know you'll overcome it and do better in your other courses.

Increases Resilience: Faith can provide the strength and courage to overcome adversity. If you're running a marathon, for example, and you cramp up, you don't let that stop you; you have the willpower to go the extra mile. Faith does the same thing for those who possess it.

V. Goal Achievement and Success

1. Enhances Motivation: Faith in one's abilities and the possibility of success can fuel motivation and drive. This is like having a never-give-up attitude even if you are two touchdowns behind in the 3rd quarter of a football game.

2. Increases Perseverance: Faith increases your drive and commitment even when faced with obstacles. For example, even after receiving several rejections from job interviews, you still have the will to continue to pursue your dream job. That's perseverance.

3. Improves Problem-Solving: A positive mindset fostered by faith can enhance creativity and problem-solving abilities. When you believe in solutions, you're more likely to find them.

I love life, embracing all its challenges and rewards, because I recognize that everything has meaning and purpose in the grand scheme of things. I look back on my life and understand why some doors were not open or why some relationships failed. I can see why those things happened during my time on earth and through my experiences. This is not to say I have all the answers to everything that's happened to me, but the answers I found are crucial to my transition from boyhood to manhood. Life is a journey that might seem like a puzzle, a maze, or even a dead end. Through maturity, self-awareness, and understanding your surroundings, you'll be better able to make wise decisions that shape your life.

With this book, I hope to help you gain a deeper understanding of yourself, increase your awareness of your abilities, and ignite a strong desire to start, restart, or get back on track in your life. I believe in you and have faith that you can do it, so let's all work toward being the best men we can be!

About the Author

Alan D. Benson is an author, entrepreneur, and educator who is passionate about helping others reach their full potential. He has written six books and is motivated by a strong desire to see his readers succeed in their lives, relationships, and careers. Throughout his career, he has taught, advised, and consulted, consistently guiding others with his experiences and insights.

A native of Louisville, Kentucky, Alan was raised with strong values and principles that he has carried into his own life and passed down to his children. His life has been marked by both successes and setbacks, which he views as valuable lessons in humility, self-discovery, and personal growth. He credits his father, Sam D. Benson, for raising and shaping him into the man he is today, and his mother, Marthella Benson, for her unwavering support and legacy of faith.

A proud member of Alpha Phi Alpha Fraternity, Inc., Alan believes that the principles and values he learned from the fraternity—including achievement, community service, and respect for women—have profoundly shaped his life and work. He is a veteran of the United States Marine Corps, an experience that taught him the importance of family, commitment, and facing fears head-on. His military service, particularly his deployment during the Persian Gulf War, was a pivotal moment of self-discovery that heightened his awareness and appreciation for life.

Through his writing, Alan shares his story so he can help others overcome obstacles by providing readers with a blueprint for purposeful, intentional living.

He believes that everyone has a special purpose, and his goal is to serve as a "change agent" who helps people shine and reach their full potential.

References

Ballantyne, David. "Healing Power of Green Space." *Municipal World* 134, no. 5 (2022): 7–9.

Barboza, Steven. "Approaching Stress with Curiosity." *American Jails*, 2022.

Clark, Dan. "Les Brown Shares His Story of Success and Becoming a Renowned Motivational Speaker." Dan Clark. January 28, 2025. https://danclark.com/les-brown-shares-his-story-of-success-and-becoming-a-renowned-motivational-speaker/.

Clear, James. "How Long Does It Actually Take to Form a New Habit?" James Clear (blog). Accessed February 10, 2026. https://jamesclear.com/new-habit.

Federal Deposit Insurance Corporation. "Deposit Insurance at a Glance." Last modified June 20, 2023. https://www.fdic.gov/resources/deposit-insurance/brochures/at-a-glance/.

Huang, Amy. "Development of a Risk Model for Lending Clubs." *International Journal of Information, Business and Management* 13, no. 1 (2021): 192–96.

Internal Revenue Service. "401(k) Plan Overview." Last modified October 24, 2025. https://www.irs.gov/retirement-plans/401k-plans.

Investopedia. "Stocks: What They Are, Main Types, and How They Differ

From Bonds." Accessed February 10, 2026. https://www.investopedia.com/terms/s/stock.asp.

Langreo, Libby. "Students Are Addicted to Screens." *Education Week*, May 11, 2022. https://www.edweek.org/technology/students-are-addicted-to-screens/2022/05.

Mosunic, Chris. "Learn How Long It Takes to Create a New Habit." *One Peloton*, April 8, 2025. https://www.onepeloton.com/blog/how-long-to-form-a-habit/.

Pew Research Center. "The American Family Today." December 17, 2015. https://www.pewresearch.org/social-trends/2015/12/17/the-american-family-today/.

Ramsey, Dave. *Financial Peace Revisited*. New York: Viking, 2003.

Selk, Jason. "Habit Formation: The 21-Day Myth." *Forbes*, April 15, 2013. https://www.forbes.com/sites/jasonselk/2013/04/15/habit-formation-the-21-day-myth/.

Stepzinski, Teresa. "Message of City's TEDx Conference." TEDx. 2016. https://www.ted.com/tedx/events/19301.

Warren, Elizabeth, and Amelia Tyagi. *All Your Worth: The Ultimate Lifetime Money Plan*. New York: Free Press, 2005.

Weintraub, Laura. "70 High School Clubs You Can Start Now." *CollegeVine*, 2023. https://blog.collegevine.com/high-school-clubs/

www.ingramcontent.com/pod-product-compliance
Lightning Source LLC
Chambersburg PA
CBHW051832150726
47998CB00001B/383